The Homestead Junction   49
Torafuku   50
Treasure Green Tea Company   51
Vancouver Urban Winery   52

Scenic Hikes   **54**

GASTOWN   58–69

18th Amendment Barber Shop   60
Bambudda   61
Brush Salon   62
Inform Interiors   63
L'Abattoir   64
Lost + Found Cafe   65
Old Faithful Shop   66
The Birds & The Beets   68
The Capilano Tea House & Botanical Soda Co.   69

Sweet Tooth   **70**

DOWNTOWN COAL HARBOUR, WEST END, YALETOWN   74–90

Ancora Waterfront Dining and Patio   76
Chambar   77
Fat Duck Mobile Eatery   78
Forage   79
Hawksworth Restaurant (Lunch)   80
Hida Takayama Ramen   81
Latab Wine Bar   82
Le Tigre Cuisine   83
Medina Cafe   84
Motomachi Shokudo   85
The Cross Design & Decor   86
The Dirty Apron Cooking School & Delicatessen   87
The Paper Hound Bookstore   88
Yaletown L'Antipasto   89
Zend Conscious Lounge   90

Granville Island   **91**

MOUNT PLEASANT   94–107

Batard Bakery   96
Bird On A Wire Creations   97
Chicha Restaurant   98
Earnest Ice Cream   99
Murata   100
Osteria Savio Volpe   101
Sips Cocktail Emporium   102
The Cascade Room   103
The Last Crumb Bakery & Cafe   104
The Narrow Lounge   106
Urban Source   107

Vancouver After Dark:
Entertainment Tonight   108
Cocktails & Bubbly   111

KITSILANO   114–125

49th Parallel Coffee Roasters   116
Barbara-Jo's Books To Cooks   117
Fable Kitchen   118
Halsa Spa   120
La Buca   121
La Quercia   122
Museum of Anthropology   123
Supermarine   124
Zulu Records   125

Beach Bum   **126**

There's a lot more to Vancouver than first meets the eye. Sure, we have breathtaking mountain views, sleek glass towers and beautiful tree-lined streets, but beyond its layers is a small town populated by passionate, dedicated, supportive residents.

Whether it's the gritty, authentic character of Hastings-Sunrise; the hard, polished edges of our downtown core; or the artistic fringes of Commercial Drive — it's the nooks and crannies that make Van City truly interesting. Often referred to as a melting pot of sorts, it's not uncommon to pass Thai, Japanese and Greek restaurants all in one city block — but knowing where is worthy of your coin is another story altogether.

We like to take the time to walk around and truly explore, and highly suggest you do the same. You can get to almost every venue in this book by foot if you have the stamina, and if not, just hop on a city bus or a bicycle — it's a wonderful way to take in different areas while getting a nice workout. With this curated guide, we hope that you're inspired to dig a little deeper into what our city has to offer.

the hunt vancouver writers

adrian harris and jeremy inglett

Adrian Harris and Jeremy Inglett are the two smiling men behind The Food Gays, a food, travel and lifestyle blog. What began as a hobby has transformed into a career for both, with the always-hungry duo now running their own digital media company. When not writing and creating stunning visuals for their blog and Instagram, you'll find them spending time with their dog Milo, who's considered the resident helper on set. Adrian and Jeremy are freelance contributors for Yahoo!, as well as the digital versions of *Food & Wine*, *The Province* and *Martha Stewart*.

Where to Lay your Weary Head   5

GRANDVIEW-WOODLAND HASTINGS-SUNRISE   10–22

Baaad Anna's Yarn Shop   12
Basho Cafe   13
Dayton Boots   14
Di Olivia Tasting Bar   15
Horses Records   16
Mr. Red Cafe   17
Odd Society Spirits   18
Platform 7 Coffee   19
Roundel Cafe   20
The Red Wagon Cafe   21
Tiny Finery   22

Farmers Markets   **23**

COMMERCIAL DRIVE   26–36

Dilly Dally   28
Full Bloom Flowers   29
Havana   30
Kin Kao Thai Kitchen   31
La Grotta Del Formaggio   32
Monarchy Boutique   33
Pulpfiction Books   34
Uprising Breads Bakery   35
Via Tevere Pizzeria Napoletana   36

East Van Beer Crawl   **37**

CHINATOWN STRATHCONA   40–53

Bestie   42
Calabash Bistro   43
Finch's Market   44
Harvest Community Foods   45
Mamie Taylor's   46
Phnom Penh   47
Space Lab   48

HOTEL BLU

Classy luxury

177 Robson Street (at Cambie Street; Downtown)
+1 604 620 6200 / hotelbluvancouver.com

Double from $255

With a central location and inviting rooms such as its exclusive two-story New York-style loft units, Hotel Blu is a contemporary oasis in the downtown core. Amenities include a 8.5 m (28 ft) indoor swimming pool, sauna and jacuzzi, as well as a fitness center to help you stay on top of your exercise routine. There's also a free downtown shuttle service so that you can do a little shopping or dining nearby, or head up Robson Street for a look at the city's most popular and historical commercial thoroughfares.

LISTEL HOTEL

Art-filled respite

1300 Robson Street (near Jervis Street; West End)
+1 604 684 8461 / thelistelhotel.com

Double from $230

One of Van City's artsiest hotels, this establishment really walks the talk. Rooms on its museum floors feature authentic Northwest Coast artwork and distinctive, custom-made hemlock and cedar furniture pieces, while those on its well-appointed gallery floors feature works from esteemed Canadian and international artists. While you're there, we recommend indulging in an unforgettable meal at Forage (see pg 79), the hotel's restaurant, where executive chef Chris Whittaker delivers his innovative take on seasonal, farm-to-table cuisine.

LODEN HOTEL

Urban waterfront retreat

1177 Melville Street (near Bute Street; Coal Harbour)
+1 604 669 5060 / theloden.com

Double from $270

Looking for a taste of modernity without the fluff?
Then this boutique hotel is a must. Kick back, relax and wash your worries away at their spa or take advantage of their complimentary cruiser bikes and go for a leisurely ride. Nearby Harbour Green Park is a lovely place to people-watch and affords a stellar water view. After your cruise around Coal Harbour, visit the in-house restaurant, Tableau Bar & Bistro, for its stellar French eats and warm, inviting atmosphere.

LODEN HOTEL

MODA HOTEL

Trendy heritage lodging

900 Seymour Street (at Smithe Street; Downtown)
+1 604 683 4251 / modahotel.ca

Double from $120

This restored hotel, built in 1908, delivers a stylish vibe at
an affordable price, and is just two minutes from the arts
and entertainment district. The refurbished lobby is stunning,
with pretty, 100-year-old mosaic tiles that give us serious
floor envy, and the rooms offer a balance of modern and funky
designs. With a chic Italian restaurant, casual sports bar,
a liquor store and UVA Wine & Cocktail Bar (see pg 111)
all connected to the hotel property, you'll barely even need
to leave the premises to have a good time.

OPUS HOTEL

Snazzy, pet-friendly boutique stay

322 Davie Street (near Hamilton Street; Yaletown)
+1 604 642 6787 / opushotel.com

Double from $440

Opus Hotel is the place to be if you're looking for something central,
but not smack in the middle of the city. Boasting spa bathrooms with
heated floors, the rooms here are painted in bright colors (likely not for
the faint of heart) and come equipped with an iPad for use on and off
the property. The hotel also offers a fantastic restaurant, La Pentola,
where you can enjoy a famiglia-style feast from their rustic northern
Italian menu. Customize your own seven or 10 course meal,
and then chow down on everything from their delicate parmesan soufflé,
to the luscious tagliatelle bolognese and succulent duck breast with
housemade spätzle.

OPUS HOTEL

grandview-woodland

hastings-sunrise

We live just on the fringes of Hastings-Sunrise in an area called Grandview-Woodland, where Vancouver's earliest industrial activity took place. The neighborhood began developing in the early 1800s when the first settlers arrived and today, their European influence remains strongly present, with many of our city's finest delis and bodegas found here. We love how accessible it is to the rest of the city – just 10 minutes to Gastown on a city bus – and we'll often make the walk into downtown from there. Hastings-Sunrise has an equally storied past. Back in the mid-19th century, it was a weekend retreat town popular amongst vacationers, local loggers and mill workers. Today, it's home to a varied and hardworking community, with a vibrant and successful commercial district, much of which is independently run.

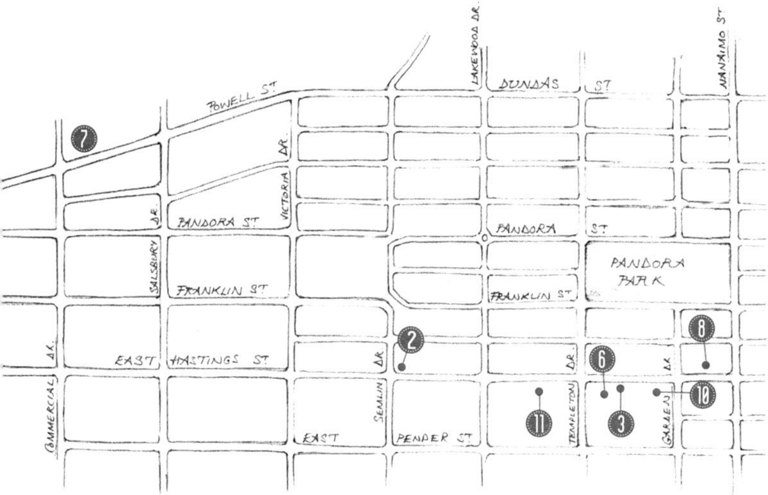

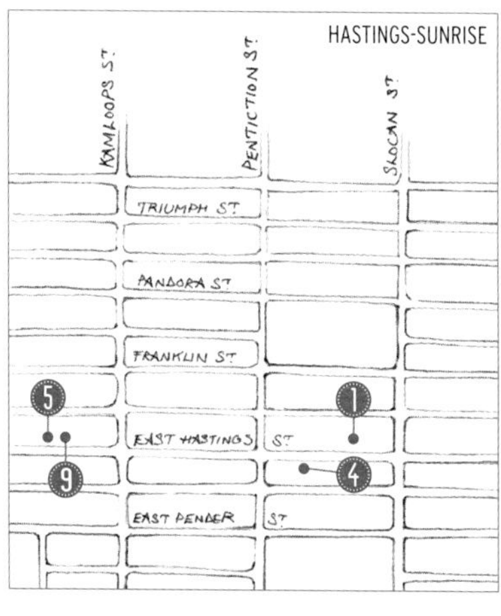

1   Baaad Anna's Yarn Shop
2   Basho Cafe
3   Dayton Boots
4   Di Olivia Tasting Bar
5   Horses Records
6   Mr. Red Cafe
7   Odd Society Spirits
8   Platform 7 Coffee
9   Roundel Cafe
10   The Red Wagon Cafe
11   Tiny Finery

BAAAD ANNA'S YARN SHOP

Unconventional purveyor of knitting supplies

2667 East Hastings Street (near Slocan Street) / +1 604 255 2577
baaadannas.wordpress.com / Open daily

For all intents and purposes, Baaad Anna's is not your regular yarn shop. While it sells some ready-to-wear items and accessories by local artisans, this knitter's wonderland is more known for its wide selection of all things knitting-related: from quality eco-friendly fibers and tools, to lessons taught in-store and online, and even equipment for rent. More than just a store, it's also a community space where you can hang out and knit without committing to a specific class. There's a kid's area stocked with toys, paper, markers and books to keep the little ones occupied while you shop. If they are keen to learn, there are workshops and birthday packages for children, too.

BASHO CAFE

Delightful Japanese eatery that's worth the queue

2007 East Hastings Street (at Semlin Drive) / +1 604 428 6276
bashocafe.com / Closed Sunday and Monday

This family-run joint offering exceptional ichiju-issai (one dish, one side)
Japanese lunch sets and creative baked goodies is no secret, with lines
snaking out the door to prove its popularity. Once you're inside, it's easy
to get lost in its charming ways as you admire the handmade crafts that
adorn the walls and tables, the reclaimed wooden furniture and its eclectic
record collection at the back of the restaurant. The tuna tataki rice bowl
is outstanding, and is the reason why this buzzing spot is a must-visit
for us when in East Van. Dessert lovers who are into anything matcha
mustn't miss the matcha latte and rotating selection of bakes including the
mochi cupcake, white chocolate brownie, espresso cookie, financiers and
madeleines – all infused with the earthy aroma and goodness of green tea.

DAYTON BOOTS

Shoemaker with a cult following

2250 East Hastings Street (near Garden Drive) / +1 604 253 6671
daytonboots.com / Closed Sunday

With fans including loggers, bikers and movie stars spanning the globe,
this iconic brand has built its reputation on rugged durability and custom,
handcrafted details. It's a business that is embedded deep within
British Columbia's logging history, with the original Dayton boot going all
the way back to 1946, and a man named C. H. 'Charlie' Wohlford. Dubbed a
first rate craftsman and problem solver, Charlie was known for his excellent
ability to fix shoes, making them better than new. One legendary, whiskey-
infused evening, Charlie was convinced by friends to start his own line of
work boots, and well, the rest is history. Today, the range includes leisure
boots for both men and women, with designs ranging from biker kicks to
urban ankle boots and lace-ups.

DI OLIVIA TASTING BAR

Specialty oils and vinegars

**2632 East Hastings Street (near Penticton Street) / +1 604 248 6999
dioliva.ca / Closed Monday**

We're lucky to live in close proximity to this gourmet haven that is home to over 50 different olive oils and balsamic vinegars imported from across the world. The entire shop is filled with glorious discoveries to whet your palate – and if you're major foodies like us, it's safe to say you won't look at such condiments in quite the same way again after visiting. Housed in stainless steel drums called fusti, shoppers are encouraged to taste the products before they buy. Think inventive and unusual flavors like blueberry, lemon, rosemary – even peach. All of Di Olivia's products are natural, preservative-free and non-GMO certified. We love using their goods when making salad dressings, or to add extra punch to sauces or dips.

HORSES RECORDS

Vinyl and poetry

**2447 East Hastings Street (near Kamloops Street) / +1 604 336 6776
horsesrecords.tumblr.com / Open daily**

Looking for a hard-to-find album from 1975, or maybe an old cassette tape from your youth? Horses Records exists for those who may be hunting the tunes of yesteryear, mixing in a distinctive personality that can only be summed up as truly East Van — friendly, slightly eclectic and laid-back.
The store features a mix of new and used LPs, poetry books, 'zines, and other pre-loved treasures. Give the cassette deck a workout, or preview an old song on the in-store record player. Owners Daniel and Katayoon are huge music and art fans, and are usually available to help with whatever you might need.

MR. RED CAFE

Stellar mom-and-pop Vietnamese eatery

2234 East Hastings Street (near Templeton Drive) / +1 604 710 9515
facebook.com/mrredvancity / Open daily

If you've never had the pleasure of tasting northern Vietnamese food, you're in for a treat at this hole-in-the-wall institution of sorts. Owned and run by Hong Duong and his wife, Rose Nguyen, Mr. Red Café serves up reliably good comfort food from their hometown of Hanoi. Don't miss their deep-fried crab rolls with rice noodles and the bánh mì pâté sandwich. When we're feeling a bit more adventurous (and hungry), we opt for the popular bun cha Hanoi: it's served on a bamboo platter with a generous pile of vermicelli, green herbs, bean sprouts, pork balls, pork belly, pickled vegetables and a deliciously pungent sweet and sour fish sauce.

ODD SOCIETY SPIRITS

Artisanal micro-distillery

1725 Powell Street (near Commercial Drive) / +1 604 559 6745
oddsocietyspirits.com / Open Thursday through Sunday

Dedicated to combining Old World distilling traditions with modern ingredients and ingenuity, this handsome neighborhood tasting room serves up an inventive cocktail menu, all made with the company's small-batch spirits including whiskey, vodka and gin. Gaze up at the huge, intriguing mural above the bar painted by artist Shwa Keirstead while you imbibe a variety of tasters available for your consumption. With a casual and modern vibe, this family-owned operation is a chill spot to kick back for a bit, enjoy a good Martini, and plan the rest of your memorable evening out on the town.

PLATFORM 7 COFFEE

Train station-inspired bean bar

**2331 East Hastings Street (near Garden Drive) / +1 604 428 1455
platform7coffee.ca / Open daily**

We love coffee, and this place never lets us down. Thanks to quality handcrafted beverages and an impressive brew bar, Platform 7 Coffee is arguably one of the most refined cafés in our city. We enjoy sitting at the back near the bar, enjoying a fat slice of pie and an Americano, or in the summer, there's a wonderful back patio space for us to relax and enjoy the rays. Exclusively serving Portland's Stumptown beans, there are pour-overs, siphons and cold brews on tap to be had. If this place doesn't make your caffeine-fueled heart skip a beat, we don't know what will.

ROUNDEL CAFE

Retro diner with wholesome food

2465 East Hastings Street (near Kamloops Street) / +1 604 253 2522
roundelcafe.com / Open daily

We started patronizing Roundel Cafe years ago for its quality breakfast, and with lunch and dinner added to the menu, we've become regulars. It has some delectable vegan and gluten-free offerings; and everything from ketchup to jam to hot sauce are made from scratch. With mindful touches like free-range eggs, beef and chicken, Roundel's menu is full of old hits with a decidedly progressive spin. When we're craving weekend brunch, we tend to go early to beat the inevitably crazy line. Don't miss the huevos rancheros, spinach and feta quesadilla, and organic beef burger.

THE RED WAGON CAFE

Comfort classics and booze

2296 East Hastings Street (at Garden Drive)
+1 604 568 4565 / redwagoncafe.com / Open daily

There's a reason why this place pulls in the crowds. The restaurant looks a bit like a run-down joint, but the rib-sticking, satisfying nosh here is what really attracts loyal hordes of foodies from all over town. Think pulled pork pancakes drizzled with Jack Daniels-spiked maple syrup; then there's the infamous Super Trucker, a massive portion consisting of two eggs, pancakes, pulled pork, crispy pork belly, homemade fries and toast. You might need to loosen your belt a notch after you're done eating, but it will totally be worth the extra calories.

TINY FINERY

Little shop of tasteful gifts

**2162 East Hastings Street (near Templeton Drive) / +1 604 569 2171
tinyfinery.ca / Closed Monday**

Enter owner and artist Stephanie Menard, the brainchild of Tiny Finery. Her wee store houses a fascinating collection of uncommon finds, including handmade accessories, ceramics and trinkets from a variety of homegrown artists. We urge you to peruse the highly curated selection of artistic cards and home décor items on display, and dare you not to take something home with you – heads up, you'll lose the dare. With custom engraving and jewelry design available, we always feel confident that our purchases here are truly one-of-a-kind.

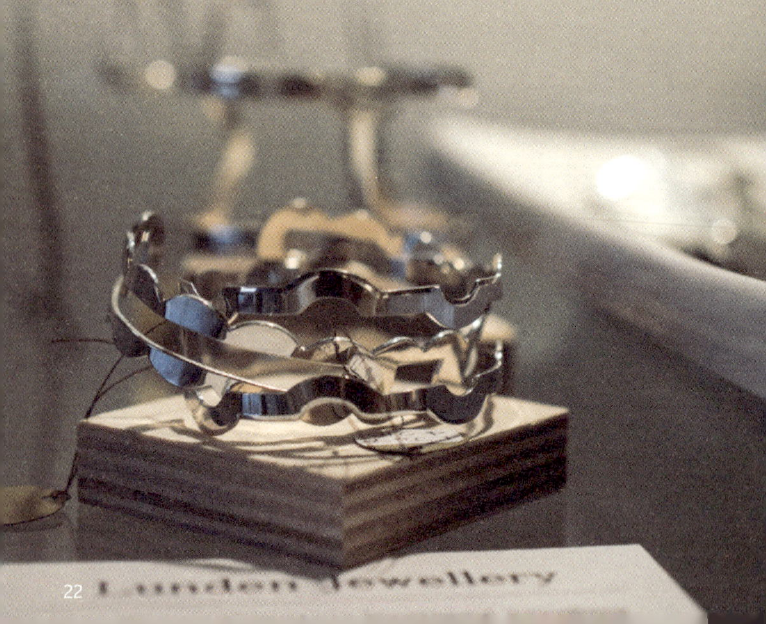

farmers markets

Fresh produce, blooms and gourmet eats

While some 80% of Canada's fruits and vegetables are imported from various parts of the US or Mexico, there's still a lot to be said about our city's thriving locavore scene. Our farmers markets are deeply woven into the fabric of Vancouver's ever-growing eat local movement, and we're truly blessed to have such a number of hardworking folks providing us with healthy, sustainable food.

We visit the markets together several times each month, particularly in the summertime, when you'll likely find one of us there every week. It's always a good idea to check the respective neighborhood market's calendar, for specific dates of operation, start time and weekly vendor lists.

Main Street Station Farmers Market, an unassuming pop-up, is found near the busy commuter intersection of Main and Terminal, right in front of the iconic Pacific Central Station building. Dozens of vendors set up shop on the east side of Thornton Park and along the sidewalk on Station Street, selling everything from homegrown produce to organic meat and dairy.

Nat Bailey Farmers Market has been running so long, it's considered the flagship of winter markets. Situated just outside of the historic Nat Bailey Stadium, it's always bustling come rain or shine. After you've done some shopping — take your pick from herbs and seasonal nursery items, to fresh farm eggs and seafood — enjoy a stroll through neighboring Queen Elizabeth Park, an urban oasis complete with manicured gardens, sculptures and a nature conservatory.

Taking place in the parking lot of Kits Community Centre, **Kitsilano Farmers Market** is overflowing with a wide selection of high quality organic meats, cheeses and artisanal bakes. Browse through original handmade crafts, and enjoy live musical entertainment by talented musicians. Bring the kiddies to have some fun at the playground and public waterpark nearby, and make a day of it.

Whoever said that Sundays were made for leisure clearly is a fan of **Mount Pleasant Farmers Market**, a lively community fixture. This beloved spring shopping destination is smack in the heart of east Mount Pleasant, and a popular hangout for residents, families and dogs alike. While you're there, treat yourself to some handmade confections. With adjacent street parking and a bike-friendly atmosphere, it's also easily accessible from the 99 B-line bus on Broadway.

West End Farmers Market is one of the smaller, more condensed markets in town, but it rarely disappoints. A hit amongst West End residents and visitors for produce, hot food and crafts, this conveniently situated artisanal strip is next to Nelson Park and adjacent gardens that are worth strolling through.

Edible flowers, herbs and luscious ripe fruits line the stands at **Trout Lake Farmers Market**, and it can be easy to spend a better part of the morning just walking around and getting inspired for our next culinary creation. This is our most-loved market, and although we may be slightly biased since it's closest to where we live, we're pretty certain you'll enjoy its lovely location and wide array of vendors. Housed just on the edge of Trout Lake, it's a great spot to sit by the water and enjoy a punnet of B.C.-grown strawberries.

Given its address, **Downtown Farmers Market** is easily the most urban pop-up of all our farmers markets and not to be missed if you're staying downtown. With a fabulous assembly of vendors, there's a staggering array of goodies to indulge in, be it farm-fresh butter and milk, or a glorious bouquet of pink peonies.

DOWNTOWN FARMERS MARKET

Queen Elizabeth Theatre Plaza
650 Hamilton Street (near West Georgia Street;
Downtown), +1 604 879 3276
eatlocal.org/markets/downtown
every Thursday (June-October)

KITSILANO FARMERS MARKET

2690 Larch Street (near Balsam Street; Kitsilano)
+1 604 879 3276, eatlocal.org/markets/kitsilano
every Sunday (May-October)

MAIN STREET STATION FARMERS MARKET

1100 Station Street
(near National Avenue; near Chinatown)
+1 604 879 3276, eatlocal.org/markets/main-st-station
every Wednesday (June-October)

MOUNT PLEASANT FARMERS MARKET

2300 Geulph Street
(near East 8th Avenue; Mount Pleasant)
+1 604 879 3276, eatlocal.org/markets/mt-pleasant
every Sunday (June-October)

NAT BAILEY FARMERS MARKET

4601 Ontario Street
(near East 30th Avenue; near Riley Park)
+1 604 879 3276, eatlocal.org/markets/winter-market
every Saturday (November-April)

TROUT LAKE FARMERS MARKET

Lakewood Drive (at 13th Avenue; near Commercial
Drive), +1 604 879 3276, eatlocal.org/markets/trout-lake
every Saturday (May-October)

WEST END FARMERS MARKET

Comox Street (near Bute Street; Downtown)
+1 604 879 3276, eatlocal.org/markets/west-end
every Saturday (May-October)

commercial drive

As one of Vancouver's most dynamic east side shopping
and dining districts, Commercial Drive (often called
"The Drive") can't be accused of being short on character.
There's a staggering amount of diversity to the businesses
here – from bodegas, delis, cafés and restaurants to
independent bookstores, florists and boutiques – most of
which are single location, and owner-run. With a heavy
European influence, the area has a strongly rooted sense
of community that is at the core of its identity.
Whenever we want to get away from the hustle and
bustle of all the shoppers, we like to take a stroll along
its charming side streets to have a glimpse of the
neighborhood's splendid Edwardian and Victorian homes,
for which the area is famous.

1 Dilly Dally
2 Full Bloom Flowers
3 Havana
4 Kin Kao Thai Kitchen
5 La Grotta Del Formaggio
6 Monarchy Boutique
7 Pulpfiction Books
8 Uprising Breads Bakery
9 Via Tevere Pizzeria Napoletana

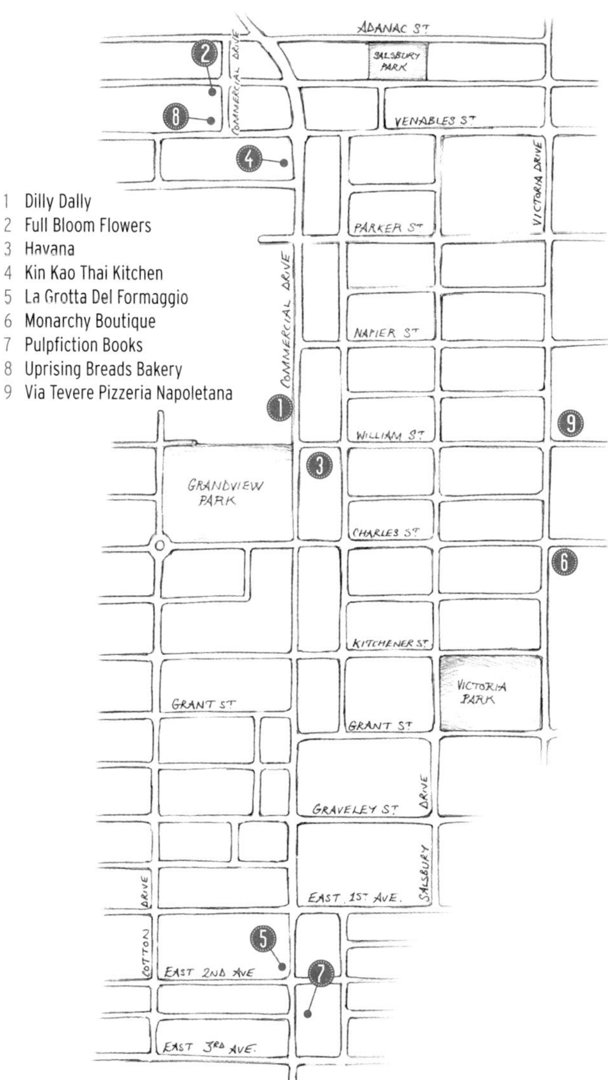

DILLY DALLY

Child's play

1161 Commercial Drive (near William Street) / +1 604 252 9727
dillydallykids.ca / Open daily

Looking for a gift for the kiddo in your life? Though we don't have children (unless you count our dog, Milo), whenever one of our nieces or nephews has a birthday, we like to pop in to this family-run toy shop and unleash our inner child. The store is full of fun and imagination, with an overwhelming selection of over 2,000 different kinds of playthings, including puzzles, books, stuffed animals and science kits. You name it, they've got it. Check out their curation of wooden toys and consider buying something thoughtful that doesn't come with batteries or buttons. We're sure this purveyor will have at least several things on your tyke's wish list.

FULL BLOOM FLOWERS

Fair trade blossoms

831 Commercial Drive (near Venables Street) / +1 604 255 1866
fullbloomflowers.ca / Closed Sunday and Monday

It may sound cheesy, but we like to surprise each other with floral bouquets, just because. If one of us is having a rough week, it's not uncommon for the other to come home with one to help brighten spirits. This cute little nook of a shop, located off the busy shopping strip, is full of enchanting blooms and plants we love to admire. Owner Michele and her staff are very friendly and knowledgeable, and their creations are always different from the average. Whether you're looking for something sleek and simple, or wild and untamed, the ladies at Full Bloom Flowers always put together memorable and eye-catching arrangements.

HAVANA

Pacific Northwest cuisine with a Caribbean influence

1212 Commercial Drive (at William Street) / +1 604 253 9119
havanarestaurant.ca / Open daily

We often cook at home, but on days when neither of us feels like it, we'll either order in, or walk over to The Drive. We discovered Havana a few years back when we were craving something a little different. Its big patio is usually packed in the summer – the perfect venue to have a drink and work on your tan. With improv comedy on Friday and Saturday (starts at 10pm; box office accepts cash only), there's nothing else quite like it in our city. The food here is rustic, and you can order everything from Puerto Rican tostones (twice-fried plantains) to the Cuban classic ropa vieja, a stew with tender beef shank, tomatoes and coconut gravy. There's even an art gallery located within the restaurant.

KIN KAO THAI KITCHEN

Fiery Thai eats

**903 Commercial Drive (near Venables Street) / +1 604 558 1125
kinkao.ca / Closed Sunday**

We like it hot, and this place is on fire. With three levels of spiciness to choose from with each of their menu items, we sometimes underestimate what their version of spicy really means (despite gentle caution from the server), and end up going a little overboard. Staples like pad Thai and pad see ew are all here and then there's their amazing deep-fried, sour-cured pork ribs — total finger food. Made with tomato and long beans, the crisp and refreshing green papaya salad is a must. Wash that all down with a pint from Strange Fellows, Dageraad or Powell Street. Okay, now we're hungry!

LA GROTTA DEL FORMAGGIO

Italian grocer and deli

1791 Commercial Drive (at East 2nd Avenue) / +1 604 255 3911
lgdf.ca / Open daily

Whenever we're on The Drive, we're methodical about working up one side of the street and down the other, making sure not to leave out any of our fancied spots along this multi-cultural stretch. A shop that we never miss is La Grotta Del Formaggio. Stepping foot into this slice of heaven is like taking a mini vacation in Italy. That's probably because Italian owner Domenico Bruzzese is all about bringing us the best of his hometown of Calabria. Once we've squeezed past the line of people custom ordering the meats and cheeses that will soon grace their panini, we're treated to a bevy of Italian staples to make our very own antipasto, primo, secondo piatto and, of course, dolce. Buon appetito!

MONARCHY BOUTIQUE

Original B.C. threads and more

1302 Victoria Drive (at Charles Street) / +1 604 873 4554
monarchyboutique.ca / Closed Sunday and Monday

If you're looking for one-of-a-kind fashion goods, Monarchy Boutique is a delightful little place to wander into. A stalwart in the area, it's been around for over 15 years, with its current owner, Cheryl, running the space for the last four. Jeremy used to ride his bike past this cool corner shop just off The Drive nearly every morning while on his way to work, often admiring the bright, eye-catching mural on the side of the store. Inside, you'll find a large selection of local fashion designerwear for women and men, and a noteworthy curation of ladies' jewelry, purses, hats and shoes to try on, and perhaps, own.

PULPFICTION BOOKS

For the love of reading

1830 Commercial Drive (near East 3rd Avenue) / +1 604 251 4311
pulpfictionbooksvancouver.com / Open daily

When we were school kids, neither of us really enjoyed reading very much. However, that's changed as we've gotten older and wiser. It's a shame there aren't very many independently owned bookstores left in our city, so we try to support the local shops as much as possible. This large, busy store stocks both new and preloved literature, including a deluge of hard-to-find content, 'zines and secondhand records to be explored in its aisles. Whenever we're searching for a captivating title to escape with, this dependable establishment has got us covered. We love that the staff are friendly and informative, too.

UPRISING BREADS BAKERY

Real good treats

1697 Venables Street (at Commercial Drive) / +1 604 254 5635
uprisingbreads.com / Open daily

One of Vancouver's oldest bakeshops, Uprising Breads Bakery, known for its multigrain, serves much more than just loaves. Jeremy used to work here, creating wholesome from-scratch products such as scones, croissants, muffins and the like, sweetened with honey or molasses and nothing else. We're partial to their lunch offerings, with some of our most-loved eats including their tomato spinach soup with parmesan cheese, and the turkey pesto baguette sandwich. If you've got a sweet tooth, try their decadent cinnamon bun or the chocolate spelt muffin.

VIA TEVERE PIZZERIA NAPOLETANA

Authentic Neapolitan pizzas

1190 Victoria Drive (at William Street) / +1 604 336 1803
viateverepizzeria.com / Closed Monday

Named after a street in the heart of Naples, where the owner's father was raised, this endearing joint has character, with an open kitchen overlooking the dining area, and an authentic wood-fire dome oven right in the middle of the room. We've been here for several birthday parties and always have a good time. The restaurant has tons of curb appeal (it's tucked away on a quaint residential street), and their scrumptious pies are some of the best in Vancouver. We're especially fond of the prosciutto e rucola. This place is only open for dinner and we suggest you arrive early to avoid a long line, as they don't take reservations.

east van beer crawl

Quench your thirst at Vancouver's hottest breweries

There's much this city does exceptionally well, and that includes craft beer. Okay, we're no Portland, but East Van is home to many of the most well-liked craft breweries in Western Canada, all with noteworthy traits.

To start our journey, let's hit up **Off The Rail Brewing Company**, a neighborhood stalwart that delivers on its promise of crafting nothing short of an excellent pint for your enjoyment. There's a wide selection for sampling — from IPAs, classic-style pale ales, red ales, porters, lagers, saisons and more — each with interesting names. Psycle Path Lager, anyone?

Walk across the street and check out **Bomber Brewing**. With its bold red sports-style logo, it's hard to miss. Started by two good friends with an affinity for hockey and hops, the microbrewery offers a seasonal rotation of pours.

Just a 10-minute walk away is **Powell Street Craft Brewery**, with a 20-seat tasting room that has everything from an English pale to a brown porter style ale to a mighty hoppy IPA — you'll be sure to leave here satisfied.

One of Vancouver's oldest established breweries, **Storm Brewing** is just another few minutes down the road. Don't let the graffiti out front scare you away. This no-frills establishment run by brewer James Walton is very industrial and bare bones but is known for its wide array of highly creative blends, including a recent limited edition concoction that sold for a whopping CAD$1,000 (US$780) per bottle. There isn't a retail area, but there is affordable booze on tap for sampling, or get a growler filled.

Next up is **Doan's Craft Brewing Company**, who put the "micro" in micro craft brewing (read: it's an extremely small set-up). With an eye-catching mural from homegrown artist Ola Vollo, the quaint 40 sq m (450 sq ft) outfit fills up quickly, so you should have no trouble making new friends here. The selection of brews changes constantly.

Rounding out our watering hole crawl is a personal favorite, **Parallel 49 Brewing Company**, arguably the most established name in our city's craft beer scene. Grab yourself a sample flight and enjoy some street food from the different food trucks usually parked outside. They'll often have a special of some kind, with crazy, daily brew flavor combinations you won't see anywhere else.

OFF THE RAIL BREWING COMPANY

BOMBER BREWING
1488 Adanac Street
(at McLean Drive; Commercial Drive)
+1 604 428 7457, bomberbrewing.com, open daily

DOAN'S CRAFT BREWING COMPANY
1830 Powell Street
(near Salsbury Drive; Grandview-Woodland)
+1 604 559 0415, doanscraftbrewing.com, open daily

OFF THE RAIL BREWING COMPANY
1351 Adanac Street
(near Clark Drive; near Strathcona)
+1 604 563 5767, offtherailbrewing.com, open daily

PARALLEL 49 BREWING COMPANY
1950 Triumph Street
(near Semlin Drive; Grandview-Woodland)
+1 604 558 2739, parallel49brewing.com
closed Sunday and Monday

POWELL STREET CRAFT BREWERY
1357 Powell Street
(near Clark Drive; Grandview-Woodland)
+1 604 558 2537, powellbeer.com, open daily

STORM BREWING
310 Commercial Drive
(at Franklin Street; Grandview-Woodland)
+1 604 255 9119, stormbrewing.org, closed Monday

chinatown

strathcona

Chinatown has seen plenty of changes over the last decade, with the prolilferation of new and culturally diverse businesses in the area. Nonetheless, there's a lot of history here if you look for it. Wander into a few traditional Chinese tea and herb shops, or indulge in a leisurely dim sum brunch at the bustling Cantonese eateries in the area. Neighboring Strathcona holds a special place in our hearts, as it's where we lived for many years. Over the last two decades, the area has undoubtedly become one of the most sought-after neighborhoods, and it's where many artists and creatives reside. You'll pass a house-turned-gallery on any given day, and there's a plethora of small studios around. While its commercial district is relatively small, we'd argue that there's much to be discovered, especially if you like exploring. It's considered one of Vancouver's oldest residential areas, and if you appreciate architecture and manicured gardens, we'd definitely suggest you take a walk through its sleepy streets, and get lost for a little while.

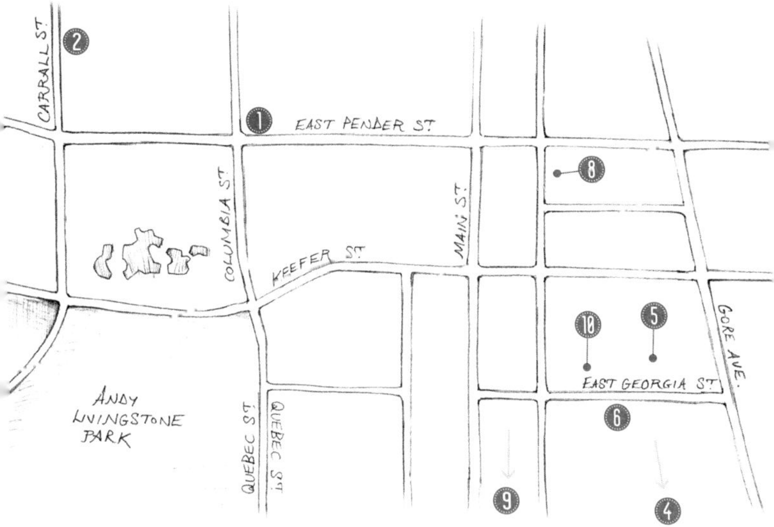

1 Bestie
2 Calabash Bistro
3 Finch's Market
4 Harvest Community Foods (off map)
5 Mamie Taylor's
6 Phnom Penh
7 Space Lab
8 The Homestead Junction
9 Torafuku (off map)
10 Treasure Green Tea Company
11 Vancouver Urban Winery (off map)

BESTIE

Best of the wurst

105 East Pender Street (near Columbia Street) / +1 604 620 1175
bestie.ca / Open daily

When you think of Chinatown, you might not think of German currywurst, and rightly so. Bestie was conceived a few years ago, and the idea of opening such a specialized restaurant in this part of town probably seemed a bit crazy but owners Clint and Dane had a clear vision. They designed the entire space from the ground up – right down to its quirky wood paneled seats, cutlery and plates. After running a successful Indigogo campaign to raise initial funds, the duo's friendly beer and sausage parlor has become our default for a bite whenever we're in the hood and looking to nosh. Treat yourself to their beef and stout banger and a freshly baked pretzel with mustard. You can thank us later.

CALABASH BISTRO

Fusion eats with great music

428 Carrall Street (near East Hastings Street) / +1 604 568 5882
calabashbistro.com / Closed Monday

Whenever we're in the mood for some laid-back Caribbean food, this place consistently gratifies. With a lively, relaxed ambience, the restaurant seamlessly fuses authentic island cuisine and twists on Western classics. One such dish is the jerk prawn and green papaya salad – a delightful combination of prawns, salt fish, green papaya and bell peppers tossed in vinagrette and dusted with tamarind coconut choka (dry-cured and roasted coconut, ground with aromatics and spices). The basement is a homey space for live music, and we recommend you try their wicked version of the Dark and Stormy cocktail, made with ginger-infused rum, angostura bitters and housemade ginger beer.

FINCH'S MARKET

Delectable sandwiches in a quaint setting

501 East Georgia Street (at Jackson Avenue) / +1 604 558 1644
finchesteahouse.com / Closed Sunday

We can't begin to tell you how much we adore this little café and grocery store. Adrian grew up just a couple of blocks away, and for over 20 years, it was a rundown corner shop, selling cigarettes and candy. That has since changed, and these days it's a relaxing hangout for the community that lives nearby. We encourage you to grab a seat at one of the intimate tables by the windows and people-watch for a while. Come hungry and order one of their housemade sarnies – our standard order is the prosciutto and pear baguette.

HARVEST COMMUNITY FOODS

Grocer and noodle joint

243 Union Street (near Gore Avenue) / +1 604 682 8851
harvestunion.ca / Open daily

This establishment prides itself on having a deep-rooted connection to its customers. It began as a community project in which a public vote by residents determined the use of the site – a grocery store and eatery – and this is where we head to whenever we're craving a hearty bowl of noodles and don't want to go downtown. We have zero problems inhaling their pork shoulder ramen bowl laced with candied bacon, gooey egg and wholesome greens. With an assortment of innovative ramen and udon dishes on their menu, there's something here for meat eaters, vegetarians and vegans alike. You'll also find locally sourced pantry items including vegetables, organic dairy products and chocolates lining the shelves.

MAMIE TAYLOR'S

Inventive Southern fare

**251 East Georgia Street (near Gore Avenue) / +1 604 620 8818
mamietaylors.ca / Open daily**

We've both had some very unforgettable meals here. When we first visited Mamie Taylor's, we couldn't help but notice their overt fondness for taxidermy. Ducks, hogs and other hunt deck the walls of the restaurant, and oddly enough, add to its charm. Tucked away off Main Street, this mod restaurant specializes in imaginative twists on staples from the American South and a killer cocktail list. Try the eponymous drink made with Scotch, lime juice, ginger beer and angostura bitters. Foodwise, we recommend feasting on the octopus jambalaya, made with Andouille sausage, okra, tomatoes and crispy chicken skin, or their classic shrimp and grits, with spicy tomatoes, chorizo and bottarga.

PHNOM PENH

Viet-Khmer dining institution

244 East Georgia Street (near Gore Avenue) / +1 604 682 5777
No website / Open daily

Its slightly unkempt exterior aside, this restaurant in the heart of
Chinatown has an upbeat atmosphere, and, most importantly, makes
some pretty tasty food: despite its location, the cuisine includes mouthwatering flavors from Cambodia and Vietnam. We come here every
couple of months to indulge, and Jeremy is absolutely obsessed with the
marinated butter beef, a savory and tangy dish he is always sure to order.
The deep-fried chicken wings are another favorite of ours – crispy on the
outside, and perfectly tender and juicy on the inside.

SPACE LAB

Where to time travel

230 East Pender Street (near Main Street) / +1 604 875 0450
facebook.com/I.Love.Spacelab / Open daily

Wandering into this fascinating little spot feels like you're in a time capsule. Brimming with mid-century industrial antiques like rotary phones, typewriters, reclaimed custom furniture and vintage housewares, this is the place to go if you're searching for a collector's item. With a large curation of one-off retro and classic audio gear, it's unlike any other vintage shop around town. Pro tip: The goods here sell quickly, so if you like it, buy it. There's also a charming espresso bar within, where you can rest your feet and enjoy a pour-over or latte.

THE HOMESTEAD JUNCTION

Bringing self-sufficiency into the mainstream

**649 East Hastings Street (near Heatley Avenue) / +1 604 568 7675
homesteadjunction.ca / Open daily**

As we've become better home cooks, we've found ourselves interested in making as much as we can from scratch. At the risk of sounding highfaluting, we get a bit of a cheap thrill out of saving a few dollars, and also being able to say we made it ourselves, which is why we love this place. Since we both love cheese, we thought it would be fun to check out their introductory cheese-making workshop. Who would've ever thought it would be so easy to make our own? Nowhere else in the city can you learn to craft everything from soap to plant-based medicine to kombucha. If you're keen, check online for up-to-date information on their courses, which range from basic to advanced.

TORAFUKU

Pan-Asian eats with a twist

**958 Main Street (near Prior Street) / +1 778 903 2006
torafuku.ca / Open daily**

The first time we dined at this minimalistic eatery, we fell head over heels for its colorful, gorgeously plated creations. With a focus on Asian fusion cuisine, every dish on its flavor-forward menu sports peculiar names you'll chuckle over, but we assure you the food is no joke. Whether it's the Dirty Birdy fried rice with chicken liver, prawns, tofu, chili, egg and brown rice, or the Rye So Messy chicken wings (without a doubt, finger-licking good), the restaurant has no problem filling up, or keeping you guessing. Go early, as they don't take bookings.

TREASURE GREEN TEA COMPANY

Chinese tea merchant

227 East Georgia Street (near Main Street) / +1 604 687 4181
treasuregreen.com / Closed Tuesday

In operation since 1981, this is Vancouver's first authentic Chinese tea shop. With an array of rare and traditional leaves in stock, the store features a number of beautifully packaged products, gift ideas and accessories. We once attended one of their classes, hosted by a second generation brew master (check their website for dates and availability), and learned about the proper method of preparing a cuppa. Treat yourself or a loved one to some of the elegant and exotic blends in stock, such as the snowy chrysanthemum, rose bud, or the dragon ball jasmine.

U OF
OIR
JAY
RIS
TRA
T-ME
GNO
(CAL
BEC

VANCOUVER URBAN WINERY

Raise a glass (or two)

**55 Dunlevy Avenue
(at Alexander Street)
+1 604 566 9463
vancouverurbanwinery.com
Open daily**

Nestled in an industrial area known as Railtown, this spectacular vintner is a diamond in the rough. The gorgeously designed tasting room carries more than 35 wines, and we often come here on a Friday evening for a glass and to savor their delish charcuterie. Interested in learning more about everything vino? Reserve a space at the winery's two-hour-long Sunday School series. If you're feeling peckish, visit their attached restaurant, Belgard Kitchen, which does a mean lunch and dinner, in addition to a wicked weekend brunch. We're big fans of the Belgard brunch burger made with B.C.-raised beef, cheese and a fried egg between a buttery brioche bun – it really doesn't get better than this.

scenic hikes

If you're hunting for breathtaking mountain views, tranquil waterfalls or thick alpine-studded trails, we've got you covered. There's good reason why they call it Beautiful British Columbia after all, and we're beyond blessed to be surrounded by such exquisite scenery right on our doorstep.

Fan of nature and wildlife? Pay a visit to **Burnaby Lake Regional Nature Park** located in the heart of Burnaby, some 30 minutes' drive east of Downtown. With seven trails, the park is home to an exceptional wildlife sanctuary, where avid bird watchers regularly spot rare breeds like bald eagles and great blue herons. Gaze at the beauty of the residential wildlife from the park's viewing tower, and pack a lunch for a casual picnic outside

Whether you're up for a brisk, sweat-inducing hike, or a pleasant stroll, **Burnaby Mountain Park** is a verdant and rugged environment spanning a staggering 576 hectares (1,400 acres). With a large network of 26 multi-use trails over 28 km (17 miles) in the Burnaby Mountain Conservation Area, the mountain boasts numerous picturesque creeks and streams where you may very well see a black bear, cougar, blacktail deer or coyote.

Sometimes referred to as Burnaby's Grind, **Velodrome Trails** ascends from the Barnet on the north side of Burnaby Mountain. Prepare your thigh muscles for a somewhat daunting 500 wooden steps before your route joins with the Pandora Trail for the rest of the climb to the top. A popular destination for solo hikers, the trek is complete with captivating peek-a-boo views that make for ideal photo opportunities, so don't forget your camera!

Another Vancouver landmark is **Stanley Park**, which features a dense forest lined with cedar, hemlock and Douglas fir trees. Located right next to the downtown core, it provides 400 hectares (990 acres) of natural West Coast rainforest and panoramic sea views, wildlife, landmark monuments, and access to the Seawall. With 27 km (17 miles) of trails, it's a beautiful place to spend an afternoon wandering.

Perched on the west side of town in the University Endowment Lands, **Pacific Spirit Regional Park**, popular with tourists and Vancouverites alike, offers 750 hectares (1,850 acres) of forest, tranquil water views, and family-friendly hiking routes that are open year-round. With low elevation paths, this is a great spot for a leisurely walk, with three different routes to choose from.

With glorious scenery and abundant wildlife, **Iona Beach Regional Park** is situated in Richmond, where the Fraser River connects with the Salish sea. Take in the dazzling and unobscured views of the Georgia Straight, and keep an eye out for some of the 300 species of birds that migrate here throughout the year.

BURNABY LAKE REGIONAL NATURE PARK

4519 Piper Avenue (Burnaby), +1 604 294 7450
burnaby.ca/Things-To-Do/Explore-Outdoors/
Shorelines---Lakes

BURNABY MOUNTAIN PARK

Centennial Way (Burnaby), +1 604 294 7450
burnaby.ca/Things-To-Do/Explore-Outdoors/Parks

IONA BEACH REGIONAL PARK

Ferguson Road (near Sea Island)
+1 604 224 5739, metrovancouver.org/services/parks

PACIFIC SPIRIT REGIONAL PARK

5495 Chancellor Boulevard (near UBC)
+1 604 224 5739, metrovancouver.org/services/parks

STANLEY PARK

Stanley Park (near West End), +1 604 873 7000
vancouver.ca/parks-recreation-culture/stanley-park.aspx

VELODROME TRAILS

Barnet Road (Burnaby), +1 604 294 7450
burnaby.ca/Things-To-Do/Explore-Outdoors/Parks

gastown

———•———

The city of Vancouver all started in Gastown. Back in 1867, the south shore of the Burrard Inlet was completely desolate, with only a private lumber mill operating in the area. History says a man name "Gassy Jack" came ashore one September day toting a barrel of whiskey, and proposed that the workers build a saloon where he would serve them drinks. The workers did just that and Gastown was soon born. After surviving a fire that nearly wiped out the area in 1886, the area was later declared a National Historic Site by the federal government. Today, Gastown still retains its original character – entrepreneurial, hardworking and colorful, with a riveting mix of new meets old. There's plenty of charm and character that's unique to this hood and we enjoy roaming its cobblestone streets, hanging out at its coffee shops and browsing the array of independent boutiques.

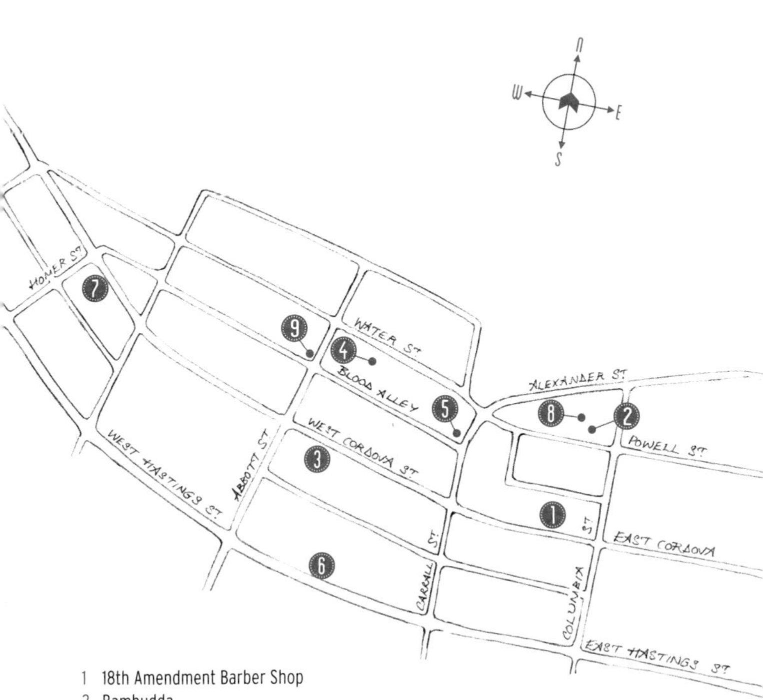

1   18th Amendment Barber Shop
2   Bambudda
3   Brush Salon
4   Inform Interiors
5   L'Abattoir
6   Lost + Found Cafe
7   Old Faithful Shop
8   The Birds & The Beets
9   The Capilano Tea House
    & Botanical Soda Co.

77 East Cordova Street (near Columbia) / +1 604 670 7798
18amendment.com / Closed Sunday

Over the last couple of years, Vancouver has seen a definite rise in the number of men's barber shops setting up shop. This ain't the dingy, old-fashioned, quick-clip of yesteryear, but rather, a mod twist on the classic boy's club, an establishment for the modern man with a fancy tavern vibe that's both masculine and mod. Take a seat in one of the shop's original 1920s Koken barber chairs and experience an exemplary hot towel shave, mo trim or a proper fade.

BAMBUDDA

Progressive Asian eats and cocktails

**99 Powell Street (near Columbia Street) / +1 604 428 0301
bambudda.ca / Closed Monday**

This dapper restaurant features innovative Chinese cuisine, with a sophisticated bar menu serving up inventive concoctions. It's the only place in town where you can order a vegan pisco sour, made with an ingenious botanical formulation that replaces the traditional egg whites. We're fond of the BBQ pork buns with pickled veggies, as well as their housemade gnocchi with wood ear mushrooms and bok choy. The food here is a good mix of experimental, small and not-so-small plates, allowing you to order an assortment of items. In the event you just can't make up your mind, go for the chef's choice menu and let fate decide for you.

BRUSH SALON

Girl, roots are for trees

**62 West Cordova Street (near Abbott Street) / +1 604 559 1737
brushsalon.ca / Open daily**

Considering our city isn't that large, we're constantly surprised by the sheer number of hair salons around. Certain areas, like Yaletown, can have up to a dozen within a few blocks' radius. It can be confusing to know who to trust with your precious locks, especially when you're stopping in from out of town. Professional and high quality work is paramount, and Brush Salon delivers on both fronts, with personable and attentive staff to boot. Offering services for both men and women, you can have a simple cut, go for color, and even do something totally different with extensions or braids. Jeremy's pretty crazy about their head massage, too!

INFORM INTERIORS

Fine home furnishings and housewares

50 Water Street (near Abbott Street) / +1 604 682 3868
informinteriors.com / Closed Sunday

Get a serious dose of eye candy at this snazzy outfit, which carries a wide
variety of good-looking items for the home, including high-end furniture
and lighting fixtures, such as the sleek and polished works from designer
Omer Arbel, as well as home décor, kitchenware and gifts. Walking into this
stunning 30,000 sq ft showroom feels akin to entering a gallery, with three
floors of alluring, tasteful creations to lose yourself in.

L'ABATTOIR

A taste of Paris in Vancouver

217 Carrall Street (near Blood Alley) / +1 604 568 1701
labattoir.ca / Open daily

Hankering for weekend brunch? Then this mod-industrial venue should appease you. With a focus on Pacific Northwest-meets-French cuisine, L'Abattoir truly lives up to its hype, from the boisterous eye-catching bar to its fetching Parisian-style floors. A loft seating area overlooks the lower level, as well as a stylish glass encased room off the back, which is the best seat in the house. Just-baked pastries are offered like breadsticks, and we suggest you nab a jelly doughnut or a scone with clotted cream while you wait for your order — they're both equally delish. We highly recommend the poached eggs with smoked pork belly, and the wild mushroom quiche.

LOST + FOUND CAFE

Charitable eats

33 West Hastings Street (near Abbott Street) / +1 604 559 7444
lostandfoundcafe.com / Open daily

Tucked away inside the old Chelsea Inn Hotel, this charismatic eatery is where philanthropy, food and art intersect. Decidedly bohemian, the airy, open room offers a funky and eclectic vibe, with phenomenal lunch and dessert items all freshly baked in-house. When they first opened, we came at least once a week for their BLT and chicken sandwiches – both worthy choices if you're hungry. While you're there, check out the crafts and postcards in their compact retail section. The proceeds help support the Dirty Wall Project Foundation, the café's non-profit partner that works in slum communities in Mumbai to provide education sponsorships, medical care and community wellness support.

OLD FAITHFUL SHOP

General store with heaps of appeal

**320 West Cordova Street
(near Homer Street)
+1 778 327 9376
oldfaithfulshop.com / Open daily**

If money was no object, you'd likely find us here on the regular. This shop, situated in a landmark 1903 building, stocks a thoughtful curation of quality lifestyle and home goods, and is the epitome of fashionable. With highly desirable objects (think homewares like luxurious throws and blankets, accessories such as Chemex coffeemakers and knife sets, books, fragrances and gourmet gifts like bourbon maple syrup) lining its handmade reclaimed wood shelves, we don't know where else in Vancouver you can buy the latest issue of *Kinfolk*, a bottle of handmade sriracha and a canvas tote all in one place.

USE A BASKET
for
EASY SHOPPING

THE BIRDS & THE BEETS

Picturesque café

55 Powell Street (near Columbia Street) / **+1 604 893 7832**
birdsandbeets.ca / **Open daily**

With two entrances (front and back), this hangout is unlike any other. A great place for food, it's also a welcome spot for people-watching and resting your tired feet. Near the front door, you're greeted by an abundance of captivating flowers and plants set against wood paneled walls — so lush you'd be forgiven for stopping in your tracks and thinking how Instagram-worthy this interior is. Serving Bow & Arrows specialty coffee, the menu includes affordably priced light bites like a poached egg and avocado on fluffy brioche, healthy grain salads and housemade pickles.

THE CAPILANO TEA HOUSE & BOTANICAL SODA CO.

Tranquil pick-me-ups

221 Abbott Street (at Trounce Alley) / +1 604 428 7632
thecapilano.com / Open daily

It's safe to say this is the only Squamish Nation-owned, plant-inspired teahouse of its kind in Vancouver. The fetching Gastown café, outfitted with exposed brick walls and a welcoming long table, is a delightful place to relax with a steamy cup of tea. Or enjoy a refreshing, artisanal soda in original flavors such as peppermint, calendula and blue cornflower, and lavender, chamomile and rosehip. Run by Michelle and Paisley Nahanee, a mother-daughter duo, the shop also serves bannock (a biscuit-type bread) topped with Local Churn Butter and East Van Jam — two Vancouver producers who make equally impressive condiments that we adore.

sweet tooth

All things chocolate

We're major chocoholics and fortunately, Vancouver has a fine selection of noteworthy chocolatiers, all of whom have their individual style. Whether you're in the mood for something simple, traditional or extra creative — we've got you covered.

Located inside the Rainier Hotel, a women's housing project, **East Van Roasters** is our city's first social enterprise chocolate shop, crafting high quality bean-to-bar products right on site. The company hires and trains the hotel's residents looking to get back on their feet, from roasting beans to packaging. The shop is a relaxed little place to sit and enjoy their irresistible drinking chocolate, and maybe nibble on a few sweets. There are yummy offerings such as their Mayan spiced truffle for sale by the piece, or opt for a box to-go and savor later. We often do both!

Beta 5 Chocolates is tucked away on a slightly obscure road just off Main Street. It isn't hard to find, but it's situated in a warehouse-style building that includes a popular commissary kitchen, also utilized by food trucks and small-batch food entrepreneurs. Once inside, you'll be treated to award-winning, artistic creations, such as the Fisherman's Friend truffle that's inspired by the menthol lozenges and their outstanding Imperial Stout and Tropical Crunch bonbons. We're big fans of the chocolate cream puffs, made with cocoa nib custard, milk chocolate mousse and a whipped dark chocolate ganache. Who can resist?

strawberry
Milk chocolate (38%),
house-made strawberry purée,
house-infused strawberry vodka.

Just east of Vancouver is **Chez Christophe**, located in neighboring Burnaby. It's a destination location — a 30-minute bus ride from downtown (catch the 135 express heading east) — but we promise you won't be disappointed. This award-winning chocolatier is known throughout the city for his enticing creations like his ridiculously ritzy salted caramel, and the delectable mango. Besides chocolates, Christophe also develops incredible pastries influenced by the seasons, and delightful French gâteaux.

Pay a visit to **Xoxolat** if you really like to geek out on chocolate. Specializing in organic and fair trade single origin and single estate chocolates, this self-proclaimed gallery of all things sho-sho-la takes deep pride in their breadth of selection. Cruise the shop's whopping 30 different truffle flavors, and admire the bevy of bars in uncommon combinations like lavender, tortilla chip and lime, or cardamom sea salt and nibs.

Chocolate Arts is always a good idea, with its delectable array of artful sweets from chef Greg Hook. The creations here are an authentic representation of our Pacific Northwest, especially the collection of eye-pleasing West Coast-influenced confectioneries, each with delicate Aboriginal design embellishments.

No chocolate tour would be complete without a visit to **Thomas Haas,** one of the city's most established patisseries. This busy café serves up a massive display of delights, from colorful, gift-worthy chocolates and caramels, to scrumptious croissants and other baked goods. Whenever we end up here, the chocolate that Jeremy always picks is the Jamaican rum truffle, made with a milk chocolate hazelnut ganache and Jamaican rum and sumptuously rolled in extra dark cocoa and sugar. Talk about a treat for the senses!

BETA 5 CHOCOLATES
413 Industrial Avenue
(near Station Street; near Strathcona)
+1 604 669 3336, beta5.myshopify.com
closed Monday

CHEZ CHRISTOPHE
4717 Hastings Street
(at Beta Avenue; near Burnaby Heights)
+1 604 428 4200, christophe-chocolat.com
closed Sunday

CHOCOLATE ARTS
1620 West 3rd Avenue
(near Fir Street; near Kitsilano)
+ 1 604 739 0475, chocolatearts.com, closed Sunday

EAST VAN ROASTERS
319 Carrall Street
(near West Cordova Street; Gastown)
+1 604 629 7562, eastvanroasters.com
closed Sunday and Monday

THOMAS HAAS
2539 West Broadway Avenue
(near Larch Street; Kitsilano)
+1 604 736 1848, thomashaas.com
closed Sunday and Monday

XOXOLAT
271 Homer Street (near Drake Street; Downtown)
+1 604 733 2462, xoxolat.com, closed Sunday

downtown

coal harbour, west end, yaletown

Downtown is made up of several distinct neighborhoods, including Gastown, Yaletown, Coal Harbour and West End. Like many cosmopolitan cities, its core is dominated these days by big box chains, restaurants and department stores. You may think it's not worth your while, but that is where you're wrong: there are a number of independently owned shops and service providers that still exist, and happily for us, are still thriving. Once you spend some time here, you'll quickly notice that this part of town is more than just an entertainment and shopping district. There are a number of offices scattered throughout the area, as well as plenty of residential condominiums that have popped up over the last couple of decades. It's a densely populated part of town, but unless you're in this hood on a Friday evening, it's usually a relatively quiet, enjoyable place to explore.

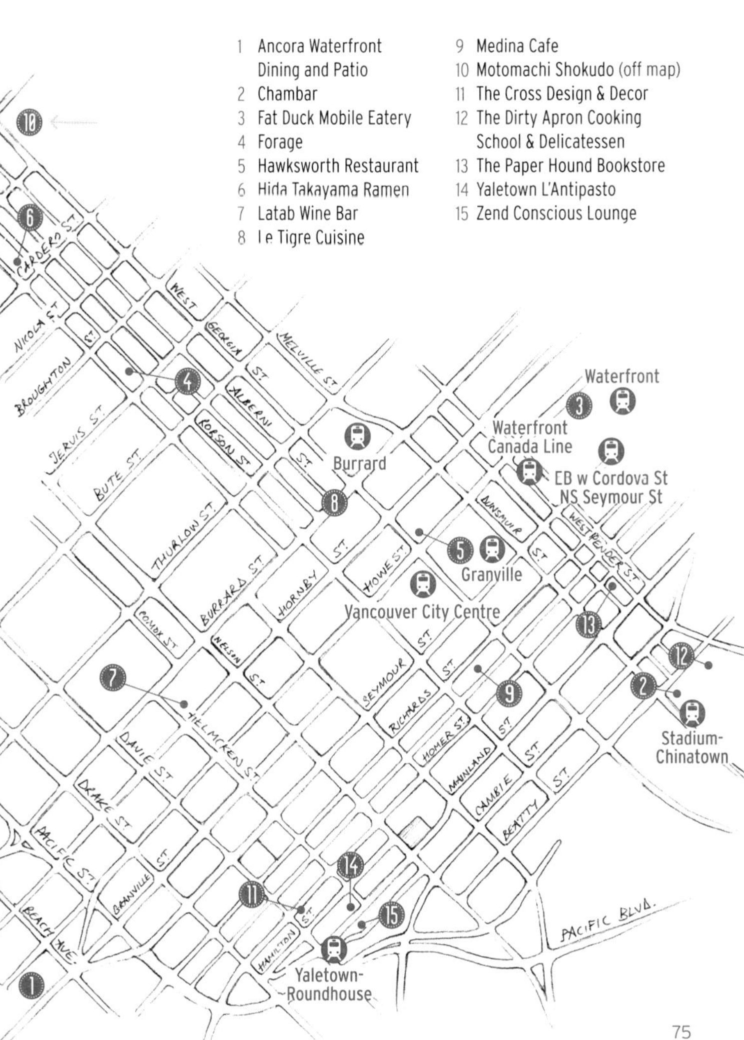

1 Ancora Waterfront Dining and Patio
2 Chambar
3 Fat Duck Mobile Eatery
4 Forage
5 Hawksworth Restaurant
6 Hida Takayama Ramen
7 Latab Wine Bar
8 Le Tigre Cuisine
9 Medina Cafe
10 Motomachi Shokudo (off map)
11 The Cross Design & Decor
12 The Dirty Apron Cooking School & Delicatessen
13 The Paper Hound Bookstore
14 Yaletown L'Antipasto
15 Zend Conscious Lounge
CARDERO ST.
NIKOLA ST.
BROUGHTON
JERVIS ST.
BUTE ST.
THURLOW ST.
BURRARD ST.
COMOX ST.
NELSON ST.
DAVIE ST.
DRAKE ST.
PACIFIC ST.
BEACH AVE.
GRANVILLE ST.
HAMILTON ST.
TIELMCKEN ST.
HORNBY ST.
HOWE ST.
SEYMOUR ST.
RICHARDS ST.
HOMER ST.
MAINLAND ST.
CAMBIE ST.
BEATTY ST.
WEST GEORGIA ST.
ALBERNI ST.
ROBSON ST.
MELVILLE ST.
DUNSMUIR ST.
WEST PENDER ST.
PACIFIC BLVD.
Burrard
Waterfront
Waterfront Canada Line
EB w Cordova St NS Seymour St
Granville
Vancouver City Centre
Stadium-Chinatown
Yaletown-Roundhouse

ANCORA WATERFRONT DINING AND PATIO

Inviting, ambient eatery

1600 Howe Street / +1 604 681 1164 / ancoradining.com
Closed Monday

We're often asked what our most-loved dining addresses are, and this place is always on our wishlist. The restaurant, tucked away at the edge of the downtown core, offers a stunning harborfront view of False Creek. Specializing in Peruvian and Japanese fusion, both the food and décor here are discriminating – from its captivating light fixtures, to the attractive presentation of the cuisine. Splurge on the eye-catching Ancora Glacier, an update on the classic seafood tower. Composed of smoked oysters, a ceviche or tartare tasting, luscious crab causa (chilled potatoes topped with Dungeness crab, kalamata emulsion, quail egg and yam chips on a bed of yellow pepper sauce), Saltspring Island mussels and fresh sashimi, you'll be one happy diner.

CHAMBAR

Sustainable dining

**568 Beatty Street (near Dunsmuir Viaduct) / +1 604 879 7119
chambar.com / Open daily**

Vancouver has become a real mecca for gastronomes in the last decade, and Chambar has garnered a remarkable reputation over the years for its ability to balance a casual yet upscale dining atmosphere with mouthwatering eats. Chef Nico Schuermans is at the helm of this operation, offering diners modern European cuisine with a farm-to-table approach. Famed for its amazing weekend brunch, you might be hard pressed to choose what to order, because everything on the menu sounds incredibly tempting. Our top pick, though, is the delish Le Burger du Chasseur, a venison burger topped with cave-aged gruyère, mushroom ragout, red wine and black pepper jam, served with roasted yams.

FAT DUCK MOBILE EATERY

Gourmet sandwich food truck

**On West Cordova Street (at Howe Street) / +1 604 831 0453 /
fatduckmobileeatery.ca / Open Monday to Friday, lunch only**

We're total sandwich guys, and could basically eat one every day if our
waistlines allowed for such indulgences. The first time we tasted the
marvelous fare from this under-the-radar food truck, which is usually found
in the downtown area, we were instantly hooked. A must try is the
Philly-style duck confit served with marinated mushrooms, pickled red
onions and truffle mayo on a buttery, toasted bun. There's often a special of
some kind on, and every order comes with a side of golden potato chips.
Be sure to check out @fatducktruck on Twitter for location updates.

FORAGE

Locavores unite

1300 Robson Street (near Jervis Street) / +1 604 661 1400
foragevancouver.com / Open daily

Sure, there are plenty of hotel restaurants around town, but few deliver on a modern diner's expectations. Attached to The Listel Hotel (see pg 6), Forage is without a doubt an exception, delivering an extraordinary approach to local ingredients, with delectable offerings such as the pan-roasted duck breast with liver mousse "cream puff", preserved fig jus and spring kale blossom. The space is warm and intimate, with an attractive bar in the center of the room. There's a small patio off the back, which is open during the warmer months, and is a special place to enjoy a glass of British Columbia-sourced beer or wine on tap.

HAWKSWORTH RESTAURANT

Dishes pretty as a picture

801 West Georgia Street (near Howe Street) / +1 604 673 7000
hawksworthrestaurant.com / Open daily

The last time we stopped in at the Vancouver Art Gallery, the works
of Henri Matisse and other modern masters were being exhibited. So it only
made sense that after spending hours taking in these iconic artworks that
we wander across the street to visit another modern master for dinner.
Not only is chef David Hawksworth's cuisine truly inspiring, but the
restaurant is also known to have an art collection that is as contemporary
as its menu. So while you're enjoying that lamb loin, perfectly roasted and
nestled against some of the freshest English peas you'll ever bite into –
see whether you can peel your eyes away from the art on your plate to take
in the works from other celebrated artists on display.

HIDA TAKAYAMA RAMEN

Handmade, slurp-worthy Japanese noodles

2F Robson Public Market, 1610 Robson Street (near Cardero Street)
+1 604 633 1884 / hidatakayamaramen.com / Closed Monday

Hida Takayama Ramen is easily one of the best kept secrets in town. This family-run, hole-in-the-wall noodle stand might be lacking a dazzling brick and mortar storefront, but we assure you it more than makes up for that with gloriously unforgettable nosh – the spicy Hida ramen and white sesame ramen are must-haves. It's also the only place in the city to make its own alkaline noodles from scratch. Their signature broth is rich in umami and MSG-free, and takes a whopping three days to make. Pro tip: ask to upsize your noodles at no charge and sit outside on the outdoor patio to avoid the harsh buzzing lights of the food court.

LATAB WINE BAR

Fabulous eats

983 Helmcken Street (near Hornby Street) / +1 604 428 7004
latab.ca / Open daily

While its locale may be rather unassuming, Latab Wine Bar must not be missed, especially if you're a fan of ingenious light bites and eco-conscious wines. Our last meal there included charred cabbage with leek and pine mushroom, sea urchin with bottarga and smoked butter on housemade raw bread, and an outstanding "vegetable egg" (you read that correctly), a vegan dish made of celeriac (the "white") and pumpkin puree (the "yolk"), served with pickled yellow foot chanterelle mushrooms and cauliflower. Explore a selection of small plates, or if you're feeling extra adventurous, opt for the Whole Shebang and savor everything on the menu.

LE TIGRE CUISINE

Inventive food truck

On Alberni Street (at Bute Street) / +1 604 613 6963
letigrecuisine.ca / Closed Monday

The food truck scene can be a tough one to navigate in any city, given its tendency for constant change and non-conformity. Chef and owner Clement Chan's yellow truck has amassed a strong following for its solid street grub with modern riffs on classical Chinese cuisine – and with no expense spared on flavor or creativity. Do yourself a favor and order the famous beet fries and the crack salad (a scrumptious toss up of Brussels sprouts, cauliflower, broccoli, kale, cabbage, capers, chili, lemon juice and parmesan). Do note that it's only in the downtown area on Thursdays. You'll find it in Cambie on Tuesdays, Railtown on Wednesdays and Granville on Fridays. Check out @LeTigreTruck on Twitter for its weekend locations.

MEDINA CAFE

Upmarket brunch

780 Richards Street (near Robson Street) / +1 604 879 3114
medinacafe.com / Open daily

Dreaming of a killer mid-morning meal? Wake up and head to this
purveyor of fine Mediterranean-inspired dining, which often attracts hordes
for its daily brunch. And when you score a seat, you'll see why. Must-tries
include the mouthwatering and irresistible build-your-own waffles,
with optional inventive toppings like white chocolate, lavender and passion
fruit, just to name a few. Perhaps you're peckish for something on the savory
side? Then get yourself the delish fricassée: two fried eggs served with
braised short ribs, roasted potatoes and caramelized onions.

MOTOMACHI SHOKUDO

Soup (and noodles) for the soul

740 Denman Street (near Alberni Street) / +1 604 609 0310
facebook.com/pages/Motomachi-Shokudo / Closed Wednesday

On a blisteringly cold afternoon, there are few foods that soothe our souls quite like a hot bowl of ramen. There's something so comforting about nestling in and slurping back that broth that just makes everything right with the world. This joint is known for its bamboo charcoal dark miso ramen, and we'll usually pop in here for a serving if it's not too busy. If the former isn't your thing, give their spicy miso ramen a try. While this isn't necessarily the speediest place in town, it's still worth a stop here, if you're a noodle fan like us.

THE CROSS DESIGN & DECOR

Posh homewares

1198 Homer Street (at Davie Street) / +1 604 689 2900
thecrossdesign.com / Open daily

When we held our first ever food styling class, we came here for all
of our props. Each time we visit is like walking into a dream store.
Irresistible home goods line the perfectly merchandised sections,
with everything from linens, plates and cutlery, to lust-worthy furniture,
bedding and more on display. While we were initially overwhelmed with
the array of items in store, we were soon picking things out like kids in
a candy store. We had our eye on the stunning bar carts and decanters,
among many other desirables, and we're pretty certain that when we get
married one day, we'll be registering here.

THE DIRTY APRON COOKING SCHOOL & DELICATESSEN

To the kitchen

540 Beatty Street (near West Pender Street) / +1 604 879 8588
dirtyapron.com / Closed Sunday

It could be said that if your apron isn't dirty by the time the food is on the table, then you really haven't thrown yourself into the making of the meal and that is absolutely the belief of The Dirty Apron Cooking School. Roll up your sleeves, don your apron and join like-minded cooks at one of their dozens of cooking classes. One very talented (and brave) instructor will take you through your paces as you whip up the dishes. When the class is done, you'll join your cooking comrades around a communal dining table, swap war stories and enjoy the fruits of your labor. Should you need to fuel up before the class, there's an in-house deli, too.

THE PAPER HOUND BOOKSTORE

Whimsical bookshop

344 West Pender Street (at Homer Street) / +1 604 428 1344
paperhound.ca / Closed Friday and Saturday

With independent literary spots being so far and few between these days, it's a place like this one that keeps the industry alive. Run by long-time book industry professionals, the shop offers a noteworthy collection of new and used titles from both well-known and independent authors. With curiously organized sections such as "wanderlust" and "books with bears", you can't help but find the place more than a little endearing. This mom-and-pop setup stocks a large selection of poetry and hard-to-find titles, and is a must-visit for any literature fan.

YALETOWN L'ANTIPASTO

Friendly Italian trattoria

1127 Mainland Street (near Helmcken Street) / +1 604 558 1174
yaletownlantipasto.com / Open daily

An authentic, family-run Italian restaurant can be hard to come by these days. Thank goodness for Yaletown L'Antipasto, a small, quaint and reasonably priced outfit that pairs delectable tastes of Italy with Old World wines. Find a table indoors or on the patio, then sit back and order up a feast. Start with beef tenderloin carpaccio and burrata caprese, before moving on to mainstays like the lip-smacking pastas. We love the lobster and crab ravioli and the spaghetti alla carbonara. Be sure to save room for dessert because this place makes a mean tiramisu.

ZEND CONSCIOUS LOUNGE

Calling all vegans (and vegan-curious)

1130 Mainland Street (near Davie Street) / **+1 778 588 6688**
zendlounge.com / **Open daily**

This Yaletown establishment offering a 100% organic plant-based menu and botanical bar is a welcome addition to the food scene. Inventive breakfast and lunch offerings are abundant here – from the sunchoke and potato rosti Benny with star anise beet cream, carrot "lox" and seasonal veggies; to its luscious kale Caesar salad with oat cheese parmesan crisps, garlic amaranth croutons and garlicky avocado dressing. The food is so scrumptious you certainly don't need to be a non-meat eater to appreciate it.

granville island

Where to cruise, eat, shop and play

We couldn't possibly let you visit Vancouver without telling you about Granville Island. With a hub of artistic and dynamic shops and services, from gorgeous waterfront dining, original boutiques and a thriving fresh food market — the energetic atmosphere is truly palpable. Buskers play outside during the summer months, which is often when you'll find us down here, soaking up some sunshine and doing a little shopping — and eating, of course. Grab an Aquabus from False Creek, Yaletown or Downtown, or catch one of many city buses that will get you here in just minutes.

Split into districts of sorts, Granville Island can feel like a slight maze to navigate initially. We'd recommend starting off with a walk through the **Maritime Market**, which sprawls along the south side of the island. There are plenty of shops stocking boating supplies and specialty clothing, and shipbuilders at work are a common sight. Take in the stunning view of the south harbor, and browse through the district's many galleries. If it's especially nice out, we'll enjoy a day in the water, renting a boat from **Granville Island Boat Rentals**. Dinner cruise more your style? Give **Accent Cruises** a try.

If you have children, you've got to stop in at **Kids Market**. The market is housed inside a 100-year-old factory, and Adrian loved coming here as a child. It's essentially a cotton candy paradise, with over 25 kid-friendly shops to explore — everything from toys, games, books and music. There's also a large indoor adventure zone to let the kiddies burn off some energy, as well as an outdoor waterpark to cool down on a hot day (Tip: The waterpark is open daily from the end of May to early September).

The Public Market is easily one of our favorite parts of the whole island. We like to grab some Montreal-style, wood-fired bagels and cream cheese from **Siegel's Bagels**, and enjoy them on the sunny waterfront courtyard, before shopping at one of the many quality farmers, bakers, butchers and fishmongers on site. This place is a foodie's paradise, and a frequent destination to hunt down hard-to-find gourmet ingredients.

Just across the street, **Net Loft** brims with shops selling everything from clothing to art supplies. If you appreciate pretty stationery like we do, don't miss **Paper-Ya**, which stocks some of the most attractive handmade paper products we've ever laid eyes on. **Liberty Wine Merchants** is our go-to when we're looking for a bottle of something really special.

We like to pop into the **Railspur District** — a cluster of industrial warehouses that have been transformed into retail spaces — when we're looking for fresh inspiration. With an incredible number of talented homegrown artists and artisans, all working with assorted mediums like glass, metal, clay and beyond — it's seemingly impossible for us to visit these merchants and not see something fascinating every time.

ACCENT CRUISES
1698 Duranleau Street (near Johnston Street)
+1 604 688 6625, accentcruises.ca, open daily

GRANVILLE ISLAND BOAT RENTALS
1696 Duranleau Street (near Johnson Street)
+1 604 682 6287, boatrentalsvancouver.com, open daily

KIDS MARKET
1496 Cartwright Street (near Anderson Street)
+1 604 689 8447, kidsmarket.ca, open daily

LIBERTY WINE MERCHANTS
1672 Johnston Street (near Duranleau Street)
+1 604 602 1120, libertywinemerchants, open daily

MARITIME MARKET
1676 Duranleau Street (near Johnston Street)
+1 604 408 0100, maritimemarketandmarina.com
open daily

NET LOFT
1666 Johnson Street (near Anderson Street)
+1 604 666 6655, granvilleisland.com, open daily

PAPER-YA
Shop 9, Net Loft, 1666 Johnston Street
(near Anderson Street)
+ 1 604 684 2531, paper-ya.com, open daily

RAILSPUR DISTRICT
Made up of Railspur Alley, Old Bridge Street and
Cartwright Street, granvilleisland.com, open daily

SIEGEL'S BAGELS
Shop 22, 1689 Johnston Street (near Anderson Street),
+1 604 685 5670, siegelsbagels.com, open daily

THE PUBLIC MARKET
1661 Duranleau Street (near Johnston Street)
+1 604 666 6655, granvilleisland.com, open daily

mount pleasant

Just 10 minutes from the downtown core, Mount Pleasant is known as Vancouver's first suburb. This part of town is steeped in rich history and housed Vancouver's thriving local brewing scene in the late 1800s to early 1900s. By the 1980s, the area was widely regarded as a ghetto: neglected and forgotten, it was overrun by drugs, homelessness and prostitution. After gentrification in the '90s, this neighborhood is now considered a centriole of independent boutiques, chic eateries, buzzing cafés and trendy late-night hangouts. It boasts a mix of commercial and residential buildings, with a diverse community spanning a wide variety of ages and cultures.

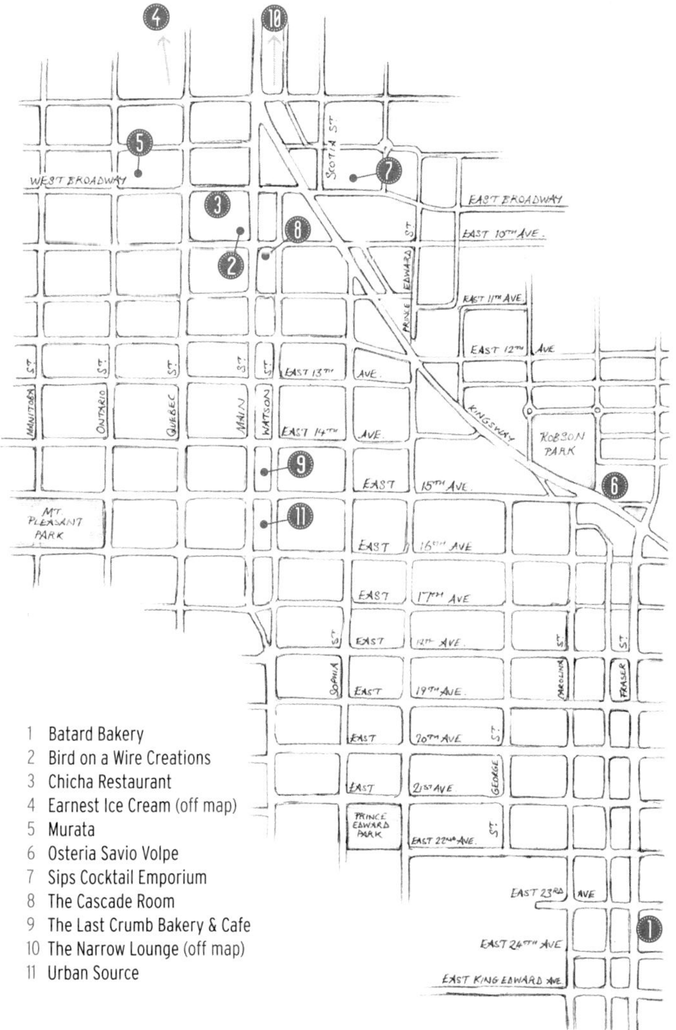

1   Batard Bakery
2   Bird on a Wire Creations
3   Chicha Restaurant
4   Earnest Ice Cream (off map)
5   Murata
6   Osteria Savio Volpe
7   Sips Cocktail Emporium
8   The Cascade Room
9   The Last Crumb Bakery & Cafe
10 The Narrow Lounge (off map)
11 Urban Source

BATARD BAKERY

Old-fashioned French boulangerie

3958 Fraser Street (near East 24th Avenue) / +1 604 506 3958
batardbakery.com / Open daily

A family-run Parisian-style bakery tucked away in a century-old building, just five minutes from Mount Pleasant, Batard Bakery is a delighfully cozy space, where the notable lack of Wi-Fi and cell reception can ultimately result in friendly chit chat between total strangers. Naturally leavened breads and scrumptious desserts are prepared daily, with a delectable array of delish treats to satisfy your sweet or savory cravings. We love their toast bar, where you get to choose from toppings like nut butter, housemade jam, or B.C. smoked salmon. There are also light lunch options such as soups and tartines. When you're done stuffing your face, peruse the retail section, which stocks artisanal preserves, spices and other pantry goods.

BIRD ON A WIRE CREATIONS

Purveyor of handmade wares

2535 Main Street (near East 10th Avenue) / +1 604 315 1188
birdonawirecreations.com / Closed Monday

Run by Kate Nagel, this homegrown shop stocks goods from local artisans, offering support and empowerment to its tight-knit community. When you walk inside, it sort of feels like a brick and mortar version of Etsy. The walls are kitted out with striking photography and paintings, and there are treasures to be discovered everywhere you look, from one-of-a-kind jewelry and accessories, to home décor items. The store also holds workshops on weaving, knitting and needle felting; just check their website for what's going on.

CHICHA RESTAURANT

Contemporary Peruvian small plates

136 East Broadway (near Main Street) / +1 604 620 3963
chicharestaurant.com / Closed Monday

Each time we dine at this modern eatery, we're roused to hop on a flight to Peru. Run by a powerhouse trio of female industry veterans, the vibe here is relaxed – the kind of place you can unwind after a long day, and knock back a few pisco sours with no judgement. Food is served in small portions, making it ideal to order multiple items to share from the extensive menu. From the refreshing chalaco ceviche (tuna, salmon, ling cod, prawns and scallops in a green leche de tigre marinade, served with pickled green papaya and crispy rocoto chili-dusted fried calamari) to the causa de atun (cilantro-whipped potato topped with soy-sesame albacore tuna, wasabi cream and passion fruit ponzu), the cuisine is bold and colorful, just like the country it draws inspiration from.

EARNEST ICE CREAM

Artisanal frozen treats

**1829 Quebec Street (near East 2nd Avenue) / + 1 778 379 0697
earnesticecream.com / Open daily**

Who says it needs to be a sunny day for something cold and utterly refreshing? Our love for this small-batch creamery started several years ago, when they had just launched their inventively flavored pints. Back then, you could only find them in selected shops in the city – but, unsurprisingly, the brand eventually took off and they now have three locations around town. Indulge in a double scoop of mouthwatering flavors such as salted caramel, oatmeal brown sugar and vegan maple walnut, or grab a frosty pint to go.

MURATA

Nippon-sourced home goods

15 East Broadway (near Ontario Street) / +1 604 874 1777
murata.ca / Open daily

Explore the Japanese philosophy of *wa*: living a quintessentially harmonious lifestyle, with principles deeply grounded in peace and unity. Stocking authentic Japanese wares like tea sets and tableware, delicate papers and intricately printed furoshiki (eco-friendly fabrics traditionally used to wrap gifts), this inviting shop likely provides whatever your heart desires. They also offer traditional ikebana (Japanese art of flower arrangement) tools and accessories, including a number of pretty handmade vases called shigaraki, which come from the famed ceramic-producing town in the Kōka District of Japan that bears the same name.

OSTERIA SAVIO VOLPE

Hearty Italian nosh

**615 Kingsway (near East 15th Avenue) / +1 604 428 0072
saviovolpe.com / Open daily**

This gem hasn't been open all that long, but has already developed a stellar reputation for winning guests over with its unpretentious and rustic approach to the deep-seated tradition of freshness and regionality of its cuisine. Choose from several housemade pastas available – we recommend the ravioli with ricotta, peas and wild onion butter or the classic spaghetti puttanesca with salt cod olives and capers – and cruise the extensive list of Italian wines to partake with your meal. Celebrating warmth, hospitality and the joy of food is what this place is all about, and we're certain you'll leave here both satisfied and yearning to return.

SIPS COCKTAIL EMPORIUM

Shaken or stirred

339 East Broadway (near Scotia Street) / +1 778 379 9747
goodsips.ca / Closed Monday

Whether you're a home bar enthusiast, or looking for an original gift for someone in your life, Sips Cocktail Emporium is just the ticket. With a sizable stock of new and vintage bar supplies for the home, this shop has everything from basic tools like shakers and glasses, to artisan bitters sourced from all over North America. Owners Darcy and Jordie are fervent about sharing their love for bespoke cocktails, and also offer informative workshops for the public, with themes such as "Intro to Bitters" and "Bartending Basics" where you can glean tips on how to make a proper drink. Bottoms up!

THE CASCADE ROOM

Familiar grub

2616 Main Street (near East 10th Avenue) / +1 604 709 8650
thecascade.ca / Open daily

A lively pick for late-night eats and drinks, this hot Main Street hangout is our go-to place when we're catching up with friends. Besides warm and unobtrusive service, The Cascade Room also offers a comprehensive craft beer and cocktail list, and top-notch eats. Think satisfying, old-school dishes; from their famed Scotch egg, to luscious bacon cheese burgers that are stacked to perfection. Check out their popular happy hour, running daily between 5pm and 7pm. Heads up though: it can get pretty crowded.

THE LAST CRUMB BAKERY & CAFE

Seriously lip-smacking sweets

3080 Main Street (near East 15th
Avenue) / +1 604 872 0195
lastcrumb.ca / Closed Monday

This nostalgic outfit run by two sisters is
where we often meet for a late lunch
or just to enjoy a cup of hot chocolate and a
treat. Besides a bevy of delectable pies and
luscious cakes made daily by hand, they also
have the most incredible cookie sandwiches
(we urge you to try the peanut butter option)
and superbly tender cheddar scallion scones.
There on a weekend? Try the brunch offerings,
which include breakfast sconewiches and
buttermilk pancakes. The mezzanine seating
is inviting and is where you might find us.
See you there!

THE NARROW LOUNGE

Hidden watering hole with fantastic eats

1898 Main Street (near Lorne Street) / +1 604 839 5780
narrowlounge.com / Open daily

Okay, so when you first lay eyes on the slightly sketchy entrance with no signage, you may be wondering what we're thinking sending you here – but hear us out. Inside you'll be greeted with one of Vancouver's hippest bars – a smallish, narrow room as its name implies. The music is good, the drinks are cheap and the food is much more elevated than you might expect from a bar. We're huge fans of their pulled pork sandwich, made with slow-cooked barbecued pork and coleslaw on a brioche bun. Sometimes, we'll opt for the Unburger Sandwich, an unctuous slice of housemade meatloaf smothered in thick, smoky BBQ sauce, baked with jalepeños and cheese, and served on a toasted baguette.

URBAN SOURCE

Alternative art materials

3126 Main Street (near East 16th Avenue) / +1 604 875 1611
urbansource.bc.ca / Open daily

Servicing all your DIY project desires, this one-of-a-kind art supply store has been serving residents for over two decades. Stocking everything from handmade greeting cards, postcards, beads and various reclaimed materials fit for just about any idea under the sun. The store partners with over 100 local industries, collecting an abundance of reusable discards, cut-offs and overstock, which are then lovingly transformed into craft materials. Fill up one of the store's three different sized bags for a set price, and let your imagination go wild!

VANCOUVER AFTER DARK:
entertainment tonight

Captivating live performances

BILTMORE CABARET

2755 Prince Edward Street (near East 11th Avenue;
Mount Pleasant), +1 604 676 0541
biltmorecabaret.com, open daily

FORTUNE SOUND CLUB

147 East Pender Street (near Main Street; Chinatown)
+1 604 569 1758, fortunesoundclub.com
open Friday and Saturday

THE CULTCH

1895 Venables Street (near Victoria Drive;
Commercial Drive), +1 604 251 1363
thecultch.com, closed Sunday

THE FOX CABARET / THE PROJECTION ROOM

2321 Main Street (near East 7th Avenue;
Mount Pleasant), +1 604 992 8180, foxcabaret.com
closed Sunday

VOGUE THEATRE

918 Granville Street (near Smithe Street; Downtown)
+1 604 688 1975, voguetheatre.com
closed Saturday and Sunday

Though there are plenty of over-crowded bars, nightclubs and the like dotted along the Granville strip to waste a Friday evening in, we tend to steer clear of those larger venues, and instead frequent places that are a bit more chill and low-key.

There's nothing like taking in a concert at **Vogue Theatre**, a fixture in our city's famed "Theatre Row" for over seven decades. The last one of its kind, it hosts a variety of performers from musicians to comedians to burlesque. Intimate in size, practically every seat in the house provides a decent view.

The Cultch is another of Vancouver's finest venues. This once-abandoned church has seen a complete refurbishment in recent years, and is a wonderful place to catch a live performance, be it theater, art or dance.

If burlesque, live music and cheap drinks sound appealing, shimmy over to **Biltmore Cabaret**, a Mount Pleasant institution that's been going strong for over 50 years. There are different musical acts ranging from DJs to tribute bands to singer-songwriters to hip hop artists performing nearly every night, with something for everyone's tastes. Over in Chinatown, there's **Fortune Sound Club**, an under the radar nightclub is where we've spent many a late night. Holding everything from hip hop nights, to live DJs and concerts, it's the ideal place for letting loose on the dancefloor.

We rarely need an excuse to enjoy good cocktails and snacks, and **The Fox Cabaret** is one of our go-to joints. Tucked inside the infamous Fox Theatre building (known as Vancouver's last adult entertainment theater), it's become a hotbed of independent culture — with live music, comedy shows, dance parties and more on the roster. Upstairs is **The Projection Room**, a cozy leopard-printed bar where you can have a drink, or three.

THE CULTCH

VANCOUVER AFTER DARK:
cocktails & bubbly

Stylish spots to sate your thirst

HELLO GOODBYE BAR
1120 Hamilton Street (near Helmcken Street;
Yaletown), no phone, hellogoodbyebar.com
closed Sunday and Monday

PIERRE'S CHAMPAGNE LOUNGE
1035 Mainland Street (near Nelson Street; Yaletown)
+1 604 761 1611, pierreslounge.com
closed Monday and Tuesday

THE EMERALD SUPPER CLUB
555 Gore Avenue (near Keefer Street; Chinatown)
+1 604 559 8477, emeraldsupperclub.com
closed Sunday and Monday

UVA WINE & COCKTAIL BAR
900 Seymour Street (near Smithe Street; Downtown)
+1 604 632 9560, uvavancouver.com, open daily

PIERRE'S CHAMPAGNE LOUNGE

UVA WINE & COCKTAIL BAR

Feeling fancy? Perhaps the lavish and sexy **Pierre's Champagne Lounge** will mitigate your VIP cravings. With premium bubbly by the glass and bottle, the swanky venue is aesthetically on point — from its handsome marble bar to its good-looking servers. Exclusivity comes with a price, however, so don't expect to get by on a tight budget here.

For those looking for something more wallet-friendly, wander over to **Hello Goodbye Bar**, just a block down the street. With no sign, you could blink and miss it, so keep your eyes peeled for the clever "hello" greeting marked on the pavement out front. Its modest entrance is through an unmarked door that leads downstairs to a remarkably trendy speakeasy; a dimly-lit, underground lounge with cool exposed brick walls, and a very solid cocktail menu. Try the Gincident, made with Tanquery, Cointreau, Chartreuse, lemon, basil and cucumber.

The wine scene is booming in Vancouver, and one place worth its weight in merlot is **UVA Wine & Cocktail Bar**. Housed inside the Moda Hotel (pg 8), the menu here is packed with imaginative craft sips created by resident bar star Lauren Mote, and a refined by-the-glass wine selection curated by general manager and sommelier Robert Stelmachuk. When we're craving something stronger, we'll order a round of Spellbound cocktails, made with whiskey, Campari and aromatic bitters.

If you dig vintage chic, you'll adore **The Emerald Supper Club**, an eclectic East Van gem smack in the heart of Chinatown. With a chill ambience channeling a mix of old-fashioned Vegas glamour meets a progressive "anything goes" attitude, the room offers a funky and alternative vibe, with zero pretense. Besides a concrete drink menu, there's great food here, too. Order the Nightsky Fizz, a whiskey, OJ, lemon, honey, egg white and Delerium Tremens concoction; and don't skip the waffle fries served with sriracha mayo.

kitsilano

In the 1800s this area was home to the Squamish people, an indigenous group who were among the first settlers in Vancouver. Today the neighborhood is often referred to by locals as "Kits," and a lively west side community mostly made up of residential districts, with two distinct commercial areas running along 4th Avenue and Broadway. Incorporating a dynamic blend of retail stores, friendly restaurants, cafés and organic food markets, it's a prime area for young families and professionals due to its desirable, high-end properties and close proximity to parks and the seaside. For us, it's the iconic beaches that draw us here.

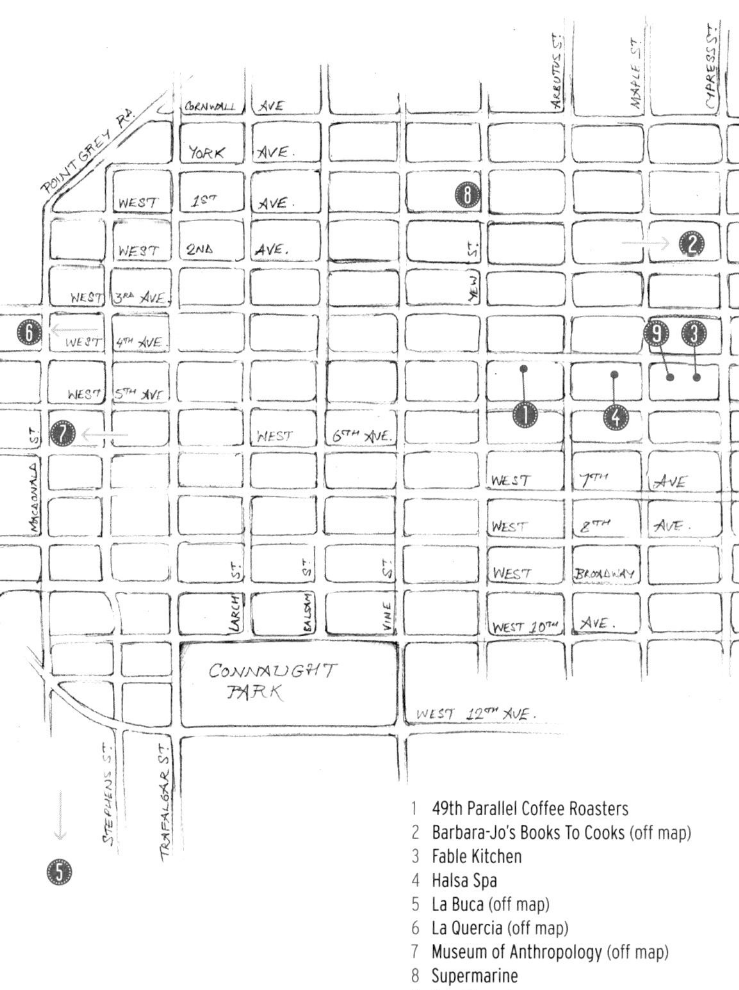

1 49th Parallel Coffee Roasters
2 Barbara-Jo's Books To Cooks (off map)
3 Fable Kitchen
4 Halsa Spa
5 La Buca (off map)
6 La Quercia (off map)
7 Museum of Anthropology (off map)
8 Supermarine
9 Zulu Records

49TH PARALLEL COFFEE ROASTERS

Caffeine and pastry hotspot

2198 West 4th Avenue (near Yew Street) / +1 604 420 4901
49thcoffee.com / Open daily

This is a superb place to pop in for your morning java, or just to kick back after a tiring day. Because what could be better than stellar coffee and exceptional doughnuts? This gorgeous Main Street café serves up the best of both, in style. With handsome wood accents and plenty of natural sunlight bathing the spacious room, seating both indoor and outside on its expansive patio, there's lots of space to unwind and enjoy a French crueller and a cappuccino or a cold brew.

BARBARA-JO'S
BOOKS TO COOKS

Dishing up something special

1740 West 2nd Avenue (near Pine Street) / + 1 604 688 6755
bookstocooks.com / Open daily

While independent bookstores are becoming more difficult to find, those that specialize in cookbooks are that much more of a rarity. Thank goodness for Barbara-Jo's Books to Cooks, a long-standing specialty shop that stocks an astounding number of foodie titles, from the mainstream TV chefs we've come to adore, to obscure, out-of-print tomes you'd be hard pressed to find elsewhere. When celebrated food personalities like Yotam Ottolenghi or Nigella Lawson have a new book to promote, they'll often come here for signings – filling up the store like the culinary rock stars they are.

FABLE KITCHEN

Homegrown eats

**1944 West 4th Avenue
(near Cypress Street)
+1 604 732 1322
fablekitchen.ca / Open daily**

One of the city's earliest advocates of farm-to-table cooking, Fable Kitchen was also among the first couple of restaurants we visited when we started food blogging. The well-appointed dining room boasts exposed brick walls, wood beams reclaimed from Vancouver's historic Cecil Hotel, and stunning hand-built shelves reserved for wine and preserves. You'll be lucky to get a table here without a reservation. That said, you can usually score a seat at the bustling bar near the front, which allows an ample view of the action from its open kitchen, and the artfully styled food being plated on the line. The menu changes with the season and memorable dishes include an excellent smoked duck breast with apple puree and cauliflower, and wild B.C. salmon with beets, confit fennel and dill yogurt.

HALSA SPA

Chill out like a Swede

**2028 West 4th Avenue (near Maple Street) / +1 604 343 1827
halsa.ca / Open daily**

Once you set foot into your sensory-deprivation float tank, you'll sense all your stresses drifting into oblivion. Influenced by Scandinavian design, this blissful neighborhood spa embraces simplicity, minimalism and functionality at its finest – delivering a truly euphoric and enchanting experience for guests to enjoy and unwind. Offering flotation therapy, infrared sauna and massage at very reasonable prices, this is one of the most pleasant and well-maintained float spas of its kind in the city. Indulge in an hour of intense, deep relaxation, and we're sure you'll look at the rest of your day with rejuvenated eyes.

LA BUCA

Personable Italian restaurant

**4025 Macdonald Street (near West 24th Avenue) / +1 604 730 6988
labuca.ca / Closed Monday**

Serving lip-smacking handmade pastas and regional specialties from all over Italy, la Buca is well-known for its seasonally spirited menu and winning service. Whether you're in the mood for a quick and low-key bite, or would like the staff to arrange a special tasting menu for your visit, the dishes here are always made with love and attention to detail. The linguine vongole with steamed clams, garlic, parsley and white wine; and the tagliatelle bolognese cooked in a rich meaty sauce are our staples. Try the chef's menu if you're up for something different.

LA QUERCIA

A taste of Italy

3689 West 4th Avenue (near Alma Street) / +1 604 676 1007
laquercia.ca / Closed Monday

An award-winning establishment deeply rooted in its heritage, La Quercia is a warm and inviting that restaurant delivers an inspiring take on northern Italian classics while embracing ingredients available in British Columbia. Customize the meal to your tastes from their enticing and seasonally focused à la carte menu, or experience the alla famiglia option and fill your table with a spectrum of different flavors from chef Adam Pegg's culinary arsenal. It's wise to make a reservation though, as the dining room usually fills up fast.

MUSEUM OF ANTHROPOLOGY

Calling all art and culture buffs

6393 North West Marine Drive (near Cecil Green Park Road)
+1 604 827 5932 / moa.ubc.ca / Closed Monday

Celebrated as Canada's foremost museum of world arts and cultures, the Museum of Anthropology is synonymous with remarkable exhibitions and evocative works. The building itself is an engineering marvel, with bold concrete beams and cascades of glass that pay tribute to the post and beam structures prominent in B.C.'s Aboriginal community. Designed in the '70s by famed architect Arthur Erickson, the museum offers a remarkable amount of native art to explore, including totem poles in the Great Hall, and more than 10,000 iconic one-of-a-kind sculptures and objects in its multitude of gallery halls.

SUPERMARINE

Sea bounty

1685 Yew Street (near West 1st Avenue) / **+1 604 739 4677**
supermarine.ca / **Closed Sunday**

Opening a seafood restaurant just a block from the Pacific Ocean seems like an obvious move, but we assure you this ain't no boring, touristy fish shack. Featuring exciting and imaginative takes on sustainable catch, this quaint 35-seat space offers an al fresco patio to lounge during a sun-soaked evening, as well as a full bar serving up craft beers and cocktails. There's even an "adult" slushie machine dispensing frozen alcohol-laced liquids like the Green Snapper – vodka, pineapple, mint and cilantro – for your imbibing pleasure.

ZULU RECORDS

Old-school album store

1972 West 4th Avenue (near Maple Street) / + 1 604 738 3232
zulurecords.com / Open daily

Do you love indie music? Does your heart skip a beat at the thought of an obscure, hard-to-find LP? If so, this is one venue you should drop by while you're in the hood. Specializing in new and used vinyl, CDs and turntables, Zulu Records has been a hotbed of music culture for over three decades. Adrian used to seek out homegrown indie gems here during his teenage years, and to this day, the place still holds the title as one of the most established independent record shops in Canada.

We're pretty fortunate to live in such a beautiful city, and our beaches are just as stunning. Though it does rain often here, when the sun makes an appearance, there are plenty of places where we can get outside and soak up every last ray.

Spanish Banks is found in the West Point Grey neighborhood, and is original in the sense that it's divided into three distinct sections. On both the east and west sides, you'll find access to the Seawall path, as well as volleyball courts, barbecues and an outdoor picnic area. Into kitesurfing, or want to take Fido for a run off-leash? Head to the extension portion of the beach. Swimming is also allowed in all areas, but do note that lifeguards are only on duty from the end of May until early September.

Just west of Kitsilano is **Jericho Beach**, which affords an unforgettable view of the North Shore mountains. Swimming is welcome on the east side, while the west side waters is reserved for sailboats and windsurfers. Surrounded by the wide open green space that is Jericho Park, the area is quite popular for kite-flying. It tends to get awfully busy here in the summer months, though, which is something to keep in mind if you're hoping for a nice, quiet afternoon.

For many people living in our downtown's West End, **English Bay Beach** (also known as First Beach) is without a doubt one of the biggest perks of the neighborhood. It's no wonder it's a favored spot for Vancouverites on a scorching day, primarily for its downtown backdrop and picturesque views. The Seawall is situated all around the beach and connecting to Stanley Park is an oasis in the middle of a metropolitan city.

We hope you get to see one of Vancouver's epic sunsets while you're here. There's probably no better place to do it than **Third Beach**. Also connected to the Seawall and nestled near Stanley Park, it has a positively tranquil vibe; ideal for a blissful day of sunbathing, or a romantic picnic for two.

New Brighton Park is our dog Milo's stomping ground. While technically a park, it features a sandy beach area, and is primarily visited by residents. Situated in East Van, the beach, in our opinion, has some of the most unforgettable panoramas of the city's North Shore and Burrard Inlet. It's a picturesque area for a walk or outdoor lunch, and the park features an outdoor pool (open during summer months). There's also a popular off-leash dog park, where you can take your pooch to burn off some steam.

ENGLISH BAY BEACH
Beach Avenue (near Denman Street; near West End)
+ 1 604 873 7000, vancouver.ca/parks-recreation-
culture/english-bay-beach

JERICHO BEACH
Point Grey Road (near Wallace Street; West Point Grey),
+ 1 604 873 7000, vancouver.ca/parks-recreation-
culture/jericho-beach

NEW BRIGHTON PARK
3201 New Brighton Road
(at North Windermere Street; Hastings-Sunrise)
+ 1 604 873 7000, vancouver.ca/parks-recreation-
culture/new-brighton-park-dog-park

SPANISH BANKS
Northwest Marine Drive, (near Tolmie Street;
West Point Grey), + 1 604 873 7000, vancouver.ca/
parks-recreation-culture/spanish-bank-beach

THIRD BEACH
Seawall (Stanley Park), + 1 604 873 7000
vancouver.ca/parks-recreation-culture/third-beach

NEW BRIGHTON PARK